Discounting in Financial Accounting and Reporting

Issues in the Literature

Acknowledgments

The authors would like to thank Wayne Upton, an observer from the Financial Accounting Standards Board, and members of the FERF steering committee, Tom Baz (chair), David Dusendschon, Winford Guin, Roland Laing, and Robert Orben for helpful comments and assistance with the study. The authors would also like to thank financial executives Mike Bohan, Rich Glazer, and Don Hollerbach for useful comments. They would like to thank their student assistants, Sofija Atanaskovic and Alex DeLuna, for their dedicated help with this project. The authors are solely responsible for the contents.

Discounting in Financial Accounting and Reporting

Issues in the Literature

Raj Aggarwal
Edward J. and Louise E. Mellen Chair in Finance
John Carroll University

Charles H. Gibson
Professor of Accounting
The University of Toledo

A Publication of
Financial Executives Research Foundation

Financial Executives Research Foundation
10 Madison Avenue, Box 1938
Morristown, New Jersey 07962-1938

International Standard Book Number 0-910586-72-1
Library of Congress Catalog Card Number 89-84511
Printed in the United States of America
First Printing

Financial Executives Research Foundation is the research affiliate of Financial Executives Institute. The basic purpose of the Foundation is to conduct research and publish informative material in the field of business management, with particular emphasis on the practices of financial management and its evolving role in the management of business.

About the Authors

Raj Aggarwal is Professor of Finance and holds the Edward J. and Louise E. Mellen Chair in Finance at John Carroll University. He teaches and does research in the areas of financial management, accounting, international business and international finance. His business experience includes work as a production engineer, as a financial analyst, and as a consultant to boards of directors and senior management of 'Fortune 100' and smaller companies in the U.S. and overseas. He holds an undergraduate degree in mechanical engineering, an M.B.A., and a D.B.A. His publications include books such as *Financial Policies for the Multinational Company, International Dimensions of Financial Management, International Business: Operating in the Global Economy, The Management of Foreign Exchange, Management Science, The Literature of International Business Finance*, and *Advances in International Planning and Forecasting*. He has also contributed many articles to scholarly and professional journals.

Charles H. Gibson is Professor of Accounting at The University of Toledo. He holds a B.A., an M.B.A., and a D.B.A. He is the author or co-author of two books, *Financial Statement Analysis: Understanding Financial Accounting Data*, and *Cases in Financial Reporting*, and contributor to the *Corporate Controller's Manual*. He has co-authored two professional development courses, *Funds Flow Evaluation* and *Profitability and the Quality of Earnings*. He has also written numerous articles dealing with financial accounting that have been published in scholarly and professional journals. He is active in several professional organizations including Financial Executives Institute, The American Institute of Certified Public Accountants, and the American Accounting Association.

Project Advisory Committee

Thomas A. Baz (chairman)
Vice President and Corporate Controller
Cubic Corporation

David W. Dusendschon
Senior Vice President
Kimberly-Clark Corporation

Winford H. Guin
Comptroller (retired)
BellSouth Corporation

Robert A. Orben
Vice President and Controller
Cummins Engine Co., Inc.

FASB Liaison

Wayne Upton
Project Manager
Financial Accounting Standards Board

Nancy K. Farlow
Publications Manager
Financial Executives Research Foundation

Contents

Executive Summary

This study is a review of the accounting literature on the use of discounting and of present value concepts in financial accounting. As indicated by exhibit ES-1, the quantity and frequency of the discussion of this topic in the accounting literature has been increasing. There are a number of reasons for the recent popularity of this topic.

First, as indicated in exhibit ES-2, interest rates, compared to their historical levels, are no longer low or negligible, and the impact of discounting can be significant. Second, users of financial accounting data are increasingly likely to have the training and knowledge required for understanding the basic nature of discounting. Third, the advent of electronic calculators and computers has made the calculations involved in using discounting in financial accounting manageable.

While the concept of discounting is part of many accounting standards, it is ignored in others. Nevertheless, the Financial Accounting Standards Board (FASB) has indicated that, without a broader investigation of the applicability of discounting to financial reporting in general, it is reluctant to expand the requirement to discount amounts recorded in the financial statements. The FASB has explicitly indicated a need for comprehensive guidance in this area and, on October 26, 1988, added to its agenda a project on interest methods to study the use of discounting.

Since a comprehensive review of the literature is an important step in any study of the appropriate use of discounting in financial accounting, this review should be of interest to businesses, accounting firms, regulators, and students of financial accounting.

Review of the Literature

The literature on discounting in financial accounting and reporting has evolved to cover a very broad array of issues and positions. It ranges from highly theoretical discussions to cookbook-like recommendations and from a strong support of the use of discounting to a strong opposition to its use in financial accounting. Our classification and organization of the literature is an attempt to deal with its complexity and range.

This study consists of six chapters, including one devoted to conclusions. The first chapter is a review of the accounting literature to 1970. We find that while the concept of time value of money has been known since at least 1800–1600 B.C., discussions among modern economists did not commence until a few hundred years ago. Discussion of the use of discounting in accounting began

EXHIBIT ES-1 **Number of Accounting Publications Discussing Discounting and Present Value, by Decade**

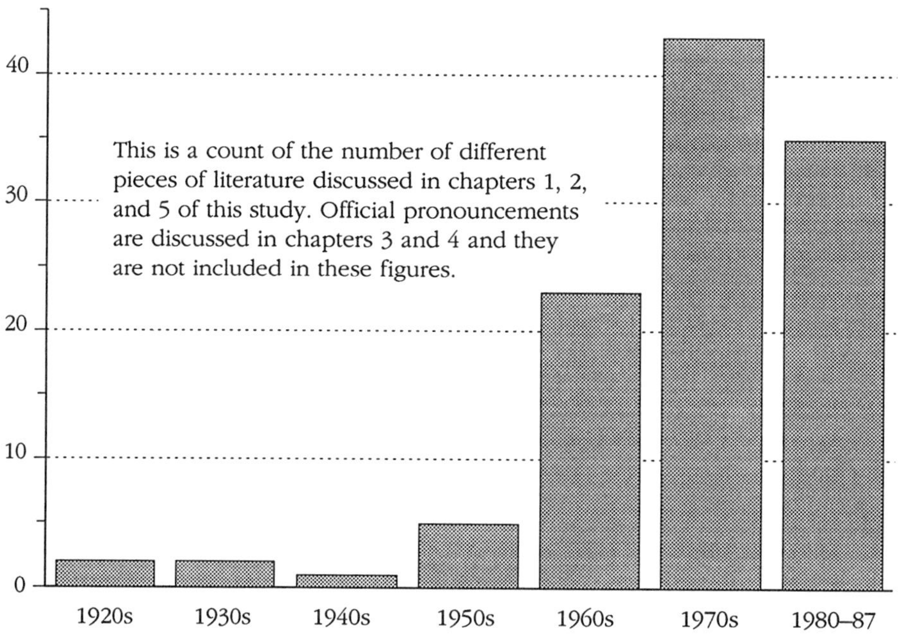

in the 1920s, but there was little interest in the topic until the late 1950s. However, it became fairly common in the 1960s.

The second chapter is a review of the discussion of discounting in the accounting literature of the 1970s and 1980s. The literature on the use of discounting in financial accounting prior to 1970 was characterized mainly by the observation that present values can provide relevant and useful information. In the 1970s and thereafter, the discussion became more sophisticated and contained detailed and complex assessments of the tradeoffs involved and the applicability of present value concepts to various areas of financial accounting.

Chapter 3 is a brief review of the literature on the use of discounting and present value concepts in studies designed specifically to offer guidance to the process of setting standards. In general, it was found that this literature recognizes the conceptual soundness of discounted present values and has recommended its use in financial accounting in a number of situations. However, efforts in this area have been characterized by ad hoc approaches without the guidance of a consistent overall framework.

Chapter 4 is a review of the use of discounting and present value concepts in accounting standards. A number of accounting standards have recommended

EXHIBIT ES-2 **Long- and Short-Term Interest Rates**

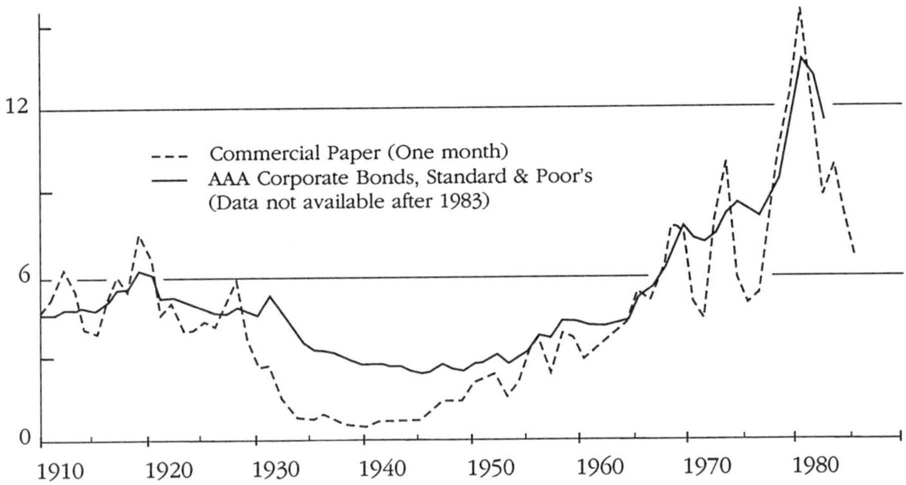

Adapted from: Board of Governors, The Federal Reserve System, *1988 Historical Chart Book*, Washington, D.C., The Board, 1988, page 96.

the use of the present value concept, others are neutral, and some recommend against their use. While the present value concept is becoming more popular in accounting standards, not all standards have considered these issues adequately and there remain a number of inconsistencies in the use of present value in the various areas of financial accounting.

Chapter 5 is a brief discussion of selected literature on the problems encountered in applying the present value concept to selected specific topics in financial accounting. This review indicates that the application of present value to specific financial accounting topics requires considerable analysis and judgment regarding its costs and benefits.

Chapter 6, "Conclusions," identifies significant issues in the application of discounting in financial accounting and provides a guide for possible further research.

The Findings

It was found that, in general, the accounting literature widely recognizes the conceptual soundness of discounted present values and has recommended its use in financial accounting in a number of situations. Still, the support for discounting is not unanimous.

Situations in which Discounting Could Be Applied

From our review of the literature, it seems that the concepts of discounting could be applied in financial accounting to determine:

1. *Fair value in initial recognition*, especially since estimates of present value are surrogates for market value. A variation is the use of time value to capitalize past money flows.
2. *Valuation following initial recognition* to account for changes that impair or add to the value of balance sheet items. Questions that must be addressed in this use of discounting include the frequency of such revaluations and the treatment of changes resulting from such revaluations.
3. *Amortization of an asset or liability*, for example, the interperiod allocation of deferred taxes or depreciation.

Issues in Applying Discounting

The literature indicates that the use of discounting in financial accounting involves the resolution of some common issues.

1. *Estimates of future cash flows.* Discounting involves estimates of the timing, amounts, and risks of future cash flows. Thus, the present value of expected cash receipts or payments generally depend upon the subjective probability of the distribution and timing of expected amounts that, by their nature, may not be verifiable. The degree of uncertainty in estimates of cash flow that can be accepted must be assessed. One approach has been to determine the classification of items (such as monetary versus nonmonetary) to which discounting should apply.
2. *Estimates of the interest rate.* Determining the rate of discount that should be used involves an estimate of the opportunity cost of the money. While the amounts and time periods for discounting can sometimes be reliably measured, in practice it is usually more difficult to assess accurately the discount rate to be used.

   Even though an objective value for the riskless discount rate might be obtainable from well-functioning and efficient capital markets, the adjustment for risk preference must be estimated. In many cases, it might be especially difficult to achieve comparability and verifiability in the estimates of the risk adjustment component of the discount rate that is suitable for a specific financial accounting application.

3. *Role of market imperfections.* Additional difficulties in the application of discounting in financial accounting may result from market imperfections. For example, it is often not possible to add together the discounted value of the individual cash flows of the separate assets of the firm to obtain the value of the firm. Thus, the application of discounting in financial accounting must also address the level of asset and liability aggregation at which discounting becomes appropriate and practical.

   These difficulties in the application of discounting in financial accounting are partly due to the interdependence of many assets and liabilities. Under some restrictive conditions (those associated with the existence of efficient markets for assets and liabilities), this problem of additivity can be overcome by using discount rates that depend only on the systematic (not total) risk associated with the asset's future cash flows. In practice, however, such conditions are rarelv, if ever, satisfied for the markets for non-financial assets. The literature review provides further details of these and related issues.

   Some of the writers in this area argue that the nature of market imperfections and market structures may also influence the application of discounting in accounting valuation. Discussed in the literature are the role of market imperfections created by transactions and information costs, such as those related to the separation of management and owners and to the interrelationships between assets or liabilities in a going concern, and their role in creating difficulties in the application of discounting to financial accounting.

4. *Estimates of materiality.* The materiality of the impact of discounting may be unclear. When the time period involved is relatively short, discounting will not usually have a material effect on the valuation of an asset or liability. For example, accounts payable would be approximately the same if shown as nominal gross amounts or as a discounted amount. Similarly, the recording of most current assets at acquisition cost may be very close to the valuation based on discounted future costs. However, when interest rates are high, discounting may have a material effect on the valuation of even current assets and liabilities.

   When the time period is relatively long, discounting will usually have a material effect on the valuation of an asset or a liability. For example, the present value of a leasehold for ten years would be materially less than the sum of ten payments paid annually during the same period.

As the discussion in this section indicates, the use of discounting in accounting valuation depends on the accuracy of projected cash flows (or values), the time period involved, and the discount rate to be used. It also depends on the role of market imperfections in influencing, for example, the appropriateness of combining discounted values of individual assets, and an estimate of the impact of discounting. The use of discounting introduces uncertainties into the accounting measurement process.

Further, the use of discounting in financial accounting has been characterized by ad hoc approaches without the guidance of a consistent overall framework. A number of accounting standards have prescribed the use of the present value concept, others ignore the concept although it seems to have relevance, and some prohibit its use. While the use of present value is becoming more popular in accounting standards, not all standards have considered these issues adequately and there remain a number of inconsistencies in the use of present value in the various areas of financial accounting. Additional research is needed in each area of financial accounting to assess the application of discounting and to develop appropriate procedures.

Conclusions

The results of this study indicate that there is substantial and widespread (though not universal) support in the literature for the use of discounting in financial accounting because its use in financial accounting can provide information that is more relevant and useful. Nevertheless, the use of discounting in financial accounting is still plagued by many inconsistencies; the application of discounting techniques in financial accounting is complicated by the conflicts between the uncertainties involved in discounting versus the need for reliability, verifiability, conservatism, measurability, and uniformity (comparability and consistency).

Thus, the controversy regarding the use of discounting in financial accounting can best be understood in the context of the tradeoffs involved in its use. Because its use involves a number of estimates, it adds to the uncertainty in accounting measures. In each application, gains in the relevance and usefulness of accounting information resulting from the use of discounting and present value concepts have to be balanced by the resulting decline in the reliability and verifiability of accounting measures.

1
Discounting In Early Accounting Literature

The concepts underlying the use of the time value of money are fairly straightforward. They are so fundamental in financial evaluation that they are potentially applicable to almost every area of financial accounting. Thus, the literature on this topic has evolved to cover a very broad array of issues and topics and ranges from highly theoretical discourses to detailed discussions of specific applications. Indeed, our knowledge of compound interest goes back at least as far as 1800–1600 B.C. and European mathematics books from A.D. 1202 onward contained problems relating to compound interest.[1] In this chapter, we review the modern literature on the use of discounting in financial reporting from the 1890s through the 1960s.

Modern Literature on Discounting Prior to the 1960s

A noted economist, Irving Fisher, is credited with formulating the concept of present value in a way that was practical for accountants and for advancing the concept within the economic community. In 1896, the Macmillan Company published, for the American Economic Association, his *Appreciation and Interest.* In Chapter 4 of that book, "Present Value," Fisher defined "present value" as the actual market price today of a future sum. He also described the present value of a perpetual annuity as its capitalized value.[2]

A significant subsequent work by Fisher, *The Rate of Interest*, was published in 1907 and revised and reissued as *The Theory of Interest* in 1930. The first chapter of the latter summarizes an earlier work by Fisher titled *The Nature of Capital and Income*, first published in 1906 and considered a significant work on the relationship between capital and income and, thus, on interest rates.[3]

Chapter 2 of *The Theory of Interest*, "Money Interest and Real Interest," is a clear explanation of the concept that monetary interest and real interest can be different, and, moreover, that the monetary rate will be influenced by the appreciation or depreciation of a currency in terms of goods. In chapter 17 Fisher tried to show that the theory of interest applies to every species of loan contract.

Other economists, including Adam Smith and John Maynard Keynes, have also contributed to the understanding of the theory of interest. However, our search of the accounting literature uncovered references mostly to Irving Fisher and John Hicks, who continue to receive most of the attention in the accounting literature. While a complete discussion of the economics of interest are beyond the scope of this study, we have included reviews of the relevant works of some other economists in the Annotated Bibliography.

Pearcy D. Leake, an accountant, considered the "investment question" in his 1912 book, *Depreciation and Wasting Assets.* He considered the annuity and the sinking fund methods of computing depreciation and concluded that the indiscriminate use of "internal annual interest" in commercial accounting, especially in connection with depreciation, is often misleading and should be discouraged.[4]

Although Fisher is credited with making significant advances in the concept of present value, John Canning, an economist and accountant, is generally credited with demonstrating the relationship of present value to accounting concepts. Canning was a supporter of Fisher's work on "interest", and his *Economics of Accountancy,* published in 1929, is credited with linking interest and present value to accounting.[5]

Chapter 8 of *The Economics of Accountancy*, titled "The Measurement of Income," is a comparison and contrast of the accountant's theory of income with the economist's theory of income. It was Canning's opinion that the most extensive and articulated discussion of income in economic literature was in the writings of Fisher. He observed that one apparent difference between the accountant's and Fisher's theory of income was Fisher's more complete "conceptual" understanding.

The one accounting theorist to make a substantial contribution between the Canning's book and the 1950s was William A. Paton. His article,"Special Applications of Discounting," published in the *Journal of Accountancy* in 1928, may actually have come out prior to Canning's book, which has a 1929 copyright.[6]

Paton's article is an extensive review of discounting in financial reporting. He took the position that discounting should apply when future sums, payable in money or its equivalent, are assured by contract. He had earlier commented, in his 1922 book *Accounting Theory*, on bond discount.[7] Thus Paton made significant contributions to the early literature on discounting in accounting.

Paton also published an article in 1936 in which he recognized the income approach to the valuation of the business enterprise. The income approach accepts the view, emphasized by many economists, that present values of production facilities represent the sum of the values of the uses which may be expected to flow from such facilities or objects through the term of their effective existence, appropriately discounted to date.[8] It is interesting that our review of the literature did not locate further references to Paton's early work on discounting.

In 1939, John R. Hicks, an economist, advanced his often-quoted definition of income in a work titled *Value and Capital*. His concept was that income is the maximum value a person can consume during a week and still expect to be as well off at the end of the week as at its beginning. Although this concept of income was stated in terms of an individual, it is thought that it could apply to a business entity.[9]

In his book *Capital and Time*, Hicks presented two caveats regarding the use of time value of money. First, he pointed out that values calculated by using interest methods are not market values and that differences between the interest rate used in calculating present values and the actual rate of return realized would lead to discrepancies in the form of capital gains or losses. Second, he cautioned that time value is continuous while interest methods often use discrete intervals to calculate value.[10]

The 1943 *Accountants Handbook*, third edition, by William A. Paton, reviews the interest method of depreciation. According to him, interest is a factor in the cost of a fixed asset, and the revenue realized from the use of the fixed asset should include the interest earned on the remaining value of the investment.[11]

The use of present value in financial reporting quickened in the 1950s. R. H. Parker attributed the earlier limited discussion of the use of present value to the profession's focus on historical recording rather than on decision making, and to the fact that the education of accountants did not include much economic theory.[12]

There were several references to the use of present value and discounting in financial accounting during the 1950s. In 1956 Hector R. Anton observed, in "Accounting for Bond Liabilities," that bond liabilities should be presented at their discounted amounts on the date of issue.[13] This, in effect, was the result of the American Institute of Certified Public Accountants, (AICPA) *Accounting Research Bulletin no. 2: Unamortized Discount and Redemption Premium on Bonds Refunded*, 1939. [14] But this standard addressed discounting only indirectly, by taking the position that a discount on bonds payable should be distributed systematically over the term of the issue.

Anton's paper noted that bond transactions involve two liabilities: one to pay a certain amount at the maturity date and the other to pay interest. He proposed that these two liabilities be disclosed separately at their discounted amount, rather than showing the principal payable less the discount or plus the premium. An example presented in the paper is as follows:

Long-term liabilities	
Bonds payable – principal (face amount, $100,000, maturing January 1, 2006)	$ 8,464.73
Bonds payable – interest (semi-annual payment, $1,500) *	54,921.16
Total bond liability	$63,385.89

*It may be desired to classify the current installment due as a current liability.

Accounting Research Bulletin, no. 2 prescribed a discounting approach based on the effective interest rate on the date of issue, and Anton also addressed discounting as using the effective interest rate on the date of issue. This was an example of recognizing discounting of the effective interest rate on the date of the original transaction, but not recognizing changes due to changes in the market rate after the original transaction date. In a 1957 paper by Norton M. Bedford, titled, "Accounting Measurements of Economic Concepts," the accountant's failure to recognize changes in the discounted value (other than amortization of bond discount or premium) was noted. Bedford reviewed the resulting divergencies between economic concepts and accounting concepts.[15]

In 1957, Thomas M. Hill published a paper presenting arguments against the interperiod allocation of income taxes. He took the position that future estimated tax payments cannot be meaningfully stated at the absolute dollar amount, but must be carried at present value. Sidney Davidson wrote a similar paper in 1958, in which he took a position against comprehensive tax allocation. Davidson contended that discounting of the deferral is required and that, if a reasonable discount rate is used, the present value of the taxes deferred is relatively small.[16]

Although the use of discounting in financial accounting was not widely observed or debated prior to the 1960s, it became a hotly debated topic during the 1960s. Discounting found its way extensively into accounting periodicals and books on theory during the 1960s. There are a number of reasons for the recent popularity of this topic.

First, compared to their historical levels, interest rates are no longer low or negligible and the impact of discounting can be significant. Second, users of financial accounting data are increasingly likely to have the training and knowledge required for understanding the basic nature of the discounting concept. Third, with the advent of electronic calculators and computers, the calculations involved in using discounting in financial accounting became manageable.

Literature on Discounting during the 1960s

In a 1961 book, George J. Staubus focused on the informational needs of investors, and developed a plan for measuring and classifying economic events. In this work, *A Theory of Accounting to Investors*, Staubus addressed the measurement of economic quantities. It was his view that measurement methods must have relevance to the firm's future cash flows. In order to have value to the investor, financial statements should present evidence of the firm's future capacity to pay investors. An emphasis on future cash receipts and disbursements was his theme as he addressed the measurement of assets, liabilities, revenues, and expenses.[17]

This is one of the most significant works emphasizing the importance of cash flow in the measurement process. Many prior articles suggesting the appropriateness of discounting in financial accounting included only a passing comment. Staubus's work was probably the first extensive article to address the appropriateness of discounting and cash flow measurements in financial accounting.

In 1962, Donald A. Corbin noted that the economists' forward-looking approach, found in managerial accounting, had not been widely adopted in the area of financial accounting. He claimed that the "revolution" involved a willingness to modify the historical cost and realization principles of accounting.

Corbin noted that Prof. John B. Canning, who was noted for his linking of accounting to economics, suggested that income should be determined by directly valuing each asset and liability at the beginning and end of each accounting period. But as Corbin observed, as of 1962, the economist's forward-looking approach had not been widely adopted in the area of financial accounting.[18]

In another 1962 paper, Stephen A. Zeff noted John R. Hicks's often-quoted definition of profit. He observed that Hicks's definition of income made reference to the discounted value of future net receipts.[19]

In still another 1962 paper, David Solomons related the market value of used assets to the present value of future benefits and found that, in the presence of interest cost and taxes, used assets are more valuable than similar new assets in terms of the present values of their future benefits.[20]

Maurice Moonitz and Louis Jordan examined a number of issues related to valuation and income in their 1963 book. They examined the effects on accounting valuation of uncertainties in transactions, such as the ability of debtors to keep their promises, the appropriate discount rate to be used, the size and timing of future money flows, and the inability to apply direct techniques of valuation. They recommended that the annuity method be used to allocate depreciation expenses.[21]

In 1964, Arthur L. Thomas attempted an in-depth review of the valuation of assets in terms of the net discounted cash flows that they are expected to generate over their productive lives. He concluded that because of the severe flaws of the "discounted services approach," it can contribute very little to financial accounting and that it can be used only in limited situations such as the valuation of receivables and other cash claims.[22]

Felix Kollaritsch published a paper in 1965 that advanced the same contention as Arthur L. Thomas 's paper. Kollaritsch stated that some recent accounting and economics literature had asserted that individual assets should be valued on the balance sheet at their future service potential value. He refuted that position and tried to show that the future service potential value is practically and theoretically unacceptable for accounting purposes.[23]

While it is widely assumed that the discounted cash flows of all assets and liabilities cannot be determined accurately, many writers nevertheless have felt that discounted cash flows can contribute significantly to financial accounting. These authors claimed that a number of assets and liabilities could be measured by the discounted value of cash flows and that the challenge was to determine how and in what situations discounted cash flows could contribute to a better understanding of financial accounting.

For example, George J. Staubus responded to Kollaritsch's article, claiming that it was interesting but contained two features with which Staubus disagreed. One was the attempt to calculate the future cash flow attributable to one part of a multipart productive facility. The other was the sweeping conclusion based on one example. Staubus contended that the measurement of assets and liabilities by discounting anticipated cash flows is one of the several useful methods of measurement and that accountants should and do employ discounted cash flow.[24]

R. J. Chambers appeared to agree with Staubus's position in a 1965 article titled "Measurement in Accounting." Chambers indicated that measurement of monetary items is simple: it would be the discounted amount to the date of the summary statement.[25]

In 1965, books on accounting theory included material relevant to the use of present value in financial reporting. It appears that the first accounting theory book, written as a college text, that discussed discounted cash receipts as a valuation concept was by Eldon S. Hendriksen.[26] He referred to John B. Canning's work as indicating that it would be desirable to have direct present value measures of all assets. Hendriksen concluded that this means that the best concept of valuation is one that is related to the expected future net receipt of funds. The degree of certainty involved in the estimate and the reliability of the estimation procedure, however, govern the extent to which it can be applied. The text also cited the Committee on Concepts and Standards Underlying Corporate Financial Statements of the American (Accounting) Association and its 1957 *Statement and Accounting Research Study, no. 3* as supporting present value as a valuation concept.[27]

Hendriksen indicated that the concept of present value requires knowledge of the amounts to be received, the discount factor, and the time periods involved. Since these factors may not be known with certainty, the method has been criticized as impractical. But he also indicated that statistical forecasting and probability techniques can often be used to convert uncertain future values into certainty equivalents and that, although discounted cash flow applies to both assets and liabilities, the amount of the discount may not be significant in short-term assets and liabilities.[28]

Robert K. Jaedicke and Robert T. Sprouse co-authored a book in 1965 titled *Accounting Flows: Income, Funds, and Cash*, which included an examination of an economic concept of income based on changes in the present value of future cash flows. The authors initially assumed conditions of certainty and unchanging price levels. Even thought these assumptions are unrealistic, authors thought that this method offers some useful insights into the real nature of income.[29]

Jaedicke and Sprouse used John R. Hicks's concept of income as an ideal type of income concept. As we noted earlier, Hicks defined income as the "maximum value a man can consume during a week, and still expect to be as well off at the end of the week as he was at the beginning." They restated this concept of income in terms of the firm "as the maximum amount that could be distributed as dividends to shareholders without contraction of the firm's resources."[30] This concept of income could be implemented by calculating the present value of future cash flows at the beginning and end of the accounting period: income would then be the difference between the two sums.

The authors pointed out that, to the extent that the decision to purchase an asset is based on the present value of future cash inflows, a present value approach is used at acquisition. For example, when a long-term bond is recorded on the basis of the proceeds at issuance, it is being recorded at present value. However, once the original transaction is recognized, accountants do not typically calculate present value: for example, fixed assets are depreciated without considering continuing changes in the present values of such assets.

Curtis Stanley introduced the concept of use value in a 1965 work titled *Objectivity in Accounting.* "Use value" is based on the idea that each potential user of an item makes a rational calculation to determine what value is provided by the item in use. For a firm this is usually the future net receipts, which should be discounted to their present equivalent.

Liabilities would be stated in terms of their present exit-market value. This would be the current number of dollars required to satisfy the liability, that is, the present value of the amount required to satisfy the liabilities at their due dates. Stanley also indicated that the interest rate used for discounting would be influenced by several factors. The rate has a subjective sense, it is a "community rate," and it is adjusted for uncertainties.[31]

In 1966, R. J. Chambers published a book titled *Accounting, Evaluation and Economic Behavior.* One of the features of this book was the emphasis on "current cash equivalent." George J. Staubus responded in 1967 with a paper titled "Current Cash Equivalent for Assets: A Dissent," which was an analysis of selected decision situations in an attempt to determine which method of asset measurement could be expected to provide the most relevant information. Staubus concluded that managers and investors both have an interest in the maximum time-adjusted cash potential. Chambers responded in 1968 by further expounding on the use of current cash equivalent.[32]

In 1966, Kermit Larson and Rudy W. Schattke criticized Chambers' *Accounting, Evaluation and Economic Behavior.* Chambers had measured the factors involved in determining the financial position of a firm by current cash equivalents. Larson and Schattke claimed that current cash equivalent (CCE) does not satisfy the requirement of additivity: that is, the CCE's of a firm's individual assets may not equal the CCE of the firm as a whole. Larson and Schattke indicated that perhaps "discounted future service potential" (the present value of future benefits) was a better possibility.[33]

Kenneth W. Lemke, in a 1966 paper, reviewed asset valuation and income theory. He noted that progress had been hindered by the interpretation of realization and by the optimum accounting definition of asset values. He suggested that a compromise could be guided by the valuation rule that each asset be valued on the basis of "sufficiently definite verifiable evidence," thus yielding what he believed to be the closest approximation to the present value of the asset's future cash flows.[34]

Homer A. Black was the author of the 1966 *Accounting Research Study, no. 9: Interperiod Allocation of Corporate Income Taxes.* Black recognized that while, in theory, discounting was relevant to all assets and liabilities recognized by tax allocation procedures, it was most likely to be applied to long-term liabilities as a practical matter. He concluded that the arguments against discounting were not convincing. Since accountants do account for present values of long-term liabilities and assets, he did not regard the argument of practicality as valid. Even though others pointed out many difficulties in doing so, according to Black, "Adoption of discounting should not be delayed by quibbles over rates . . . [and] an appropriate rate can be selected once it is decided to discount."[35]

In 1967, Robert R. Sterling commented that accounting is a discipline without any cohesive, unified theory of valuation and that the valuation methods being used varied widely for a wide variety of reasons. Many accountants consider historical cost to be objective, but Sterling suspected that present values would vary less between firms than do historical costs. He concluded that present value was likely more objective than is generally accepted. [36]

In 1968, Sybil C. Mobley suggested that a Statement of Financial Condition include a column headed "Costs" and another column headed "Projected Values." She contended that the estimated values would be a measure of current financial worth and would be useful in supporting applications for loans, making comparisons between firms, and in evaluating asset appreciation.[37] Her article did not directly address the use of present value, but the concept could be one of the methods of determining "projected values."

R. H. Parker authored "Discounted Cash Flow in Historical Perspective" in 1968. He noted that discounted cash flow has its roots in compound interest, actuarial science, engineering economy, and capital theory.[38]

In1969, Paul Rosenfield suggested that accounting turn its attention away from an irrelevant variable, replacement prices, to a search for a relevant variable which could be measured currently, suggesting present and future selling prices as two possibilities. [39]

The American Accounting Association appointed a Committee on External Reporting which authored a report titled "An Evaluation of External Reporting Practices: A Report of the 1966–68 Committee on External Reporting." This report suggested that the present value method of valuing securities was widely accepted as useful because of the importance attached by investors to the firm's future cash flows.

The committee arrived at a dividend prediction model that emphasized the firm's future cash flows both from continued operations and from changes in its asset and liability positions. The report supported the use of the present value of future cash flows related to assets and liabilities as the most relevant measure for investment decisions.[40]

Conclusions

The literature reviewed in this chapter indicates that, while the concept of discounting is not new, the idea of using it in financial reporting is relatively recent. The 1928 work by William A. Paton and the 1929 work by John B. Canning are generally considered the first major works to link interest and present value to accounting. George J. Staubus has also been one of the leading advocates of using present value in financial reporting.

It was not until the 1960s that the use of present value in financial reporting became a popular topic of discussion. Some attribute the lack of prior discussion of the use of present value in financial reporting to the accounting profession's preoccupation with historical recording and to the fact that the education of accountants did not include much economic theory.

The 1960s were a period when discussion of the use of present value in financial reporting was more accepted. The important issues then became the nature of the procedures used and discussion of when it is proper to use present value in financial reporting. And, with the advent of electronic calculators and computers, the calculations involved in using discounting in financial accounting became manageable.

Notes

1. R. H. Parker, "Discounted Cash Flow in Historical Perspective," *Journal of Accounting Research* 6, no. 1 (Spring 1968); 58, 59.
2. Irving Fisher, *Appreciation and Interest: A Study for the American Economic Association*, (New York: Macmillan, 1896), 20, 21.
3. ——— *The Theory of Interest* (New York: Macmillan,1930).
4. Percy D. Leake, *Depreciation and Wasting Assets and Their Treatment in Computing Annual Profit & Loss*, (London: Henry Good & Son, 1912): 66.
5. John B. Canning, *The Economics of Accountancy* (New York: Ronald Press, 1929).

6. William A. Paton, "Special Applications of Discounting," *Journal of Accountancy*, October 1928, 270–82.

7. ———, *Accounting Theory*, (New York, Ronald Press, 1922).

8. ———, "Valuation of the Business Enterprise," *The Accounting Review* 11, no. 1 (March 1936), p. 27.

9. John Hicks, *Value and Capital* (Oxford: Clarendon Press,1939), 172.

10. ———, *Capital and Time: A Neo-Austrian Theory* (New York: Oxford University Press,1973).

11. William A. Paton, *Accountants Handbook*, 3d ed. (New York: Ronald Press, 1943).

12. Parker, "Discounted Cash Flow," 70.

13. Hector R. Anton, "Accounting for Bond Liabilities," *Journal of Accountancy*, September 1956, 53.

14. American Institute of Certified Public Accountants (AICPA), *Accounting Research Bulletin, no. 2: Unamortized Discount and Redemption Premium on Bonds Refunded* (New York: AICPA, 1939).

15. Norton M. Bedford, "Accounting Measurements of Economic Concepts," *Journal of Accountancy*, May 1957, 57.

16. Thomas M. Hill, "Some Arguments against the Inter-Period Allocation of Income Taxes," *Accounting Review* 32, no. 3 (July1957): 360; Sidney Davidson, "Accelerated Depreciation and the Allocation of Income Taxes," *Accounting Review* 33, no. 2 (April 1958): 179.

17. George J. Staubus, *A Theory of Accounting to Investors* (Berkeley: University of California Press, 1961).

18. Donald A. Corbin, "The Revolution In Accounting," *Accounting Review* 37, no. 4 (October1962): 626, 629.

19. Stephen A. Zeff, "Replacement Cost: Member of the Family, Welcome Guest, or Intruder?" *Accounting Review* 37, no. 4 (October1962): 620.

20. David Solomons, "The Determination of Asset Values," *Journal of Business* 35, no. 1 (January 1962): 28–42.

21. Maurice Moonitz and Louis Jordan, *Accounting: An Analysis of Its Problems* (New York: Holt, Rinehart and Winston, 1963).

22. Arthur L. Thomas, "Discounted Services Again: The Homogeneity Problem," *Accounting Review* 39, no. 1 (January1964): 11.

23. Felix P. Kollaritsch, "Future Service Potential Value," *The Journal of Accountancy,* February 1965, 57.

24. George J. Staubus, "Letters to the Journal," *The Journal of Accountancy*, July 1965, 17–18.

25. R. J. Chambers, "Measurement in Accounting," *Journal of Accounting Research* 3, (Spring 1965): 54.

26. Eldon S. Hendriksen, *Accounting Theory* (Homewood, Ill.: Richard D. Irwin, 1965).

27. John B. Canning, *The Economics of Accountancy* (New York, Ronald Press); Committee on Accounting Concepts and Standards, *Accounting and Reporting Standards for Corporate Financial Statements* (Columbus: American Accounting Association, 1957).

28. Hendriksen, *Accounting Theory.*

29. Robert K. Jaedicke and Robert T. Sprouse, *Accounting Flows: Income, Funds, and Cash* (Englewood Cliffs: N.J.: Prentice-Hall, 1965).

30. Ibid, 19.

31. Curtis Holt Stanley, *Objectivity in Accounting* (Ann Arbor, Mich.: University of Michigan, 1965).

32. R. J. Chambers, *Accounting, Evaluation, and Economic Behavior* (Englewood Cliffs, N.J.: Prentice-Hall, 1966); George J. Staubus, "Current Cash Equivalent for Assets: A Dissent," *Accounting Review* 42, no. 4 (October 1967): 650–61; R. J. Chambers, "Measures and Values: A Reply to Professor Staubus," *Accounting Review* 43, no. 2 (April 1968): 239–47.

33. Kermit Larson and Rudy W. Schattke, "Current Cash Equivalents, Additivity, and Financial Action," *Accounting Review* 41, no. 4 (October 1966): 641.

34. Kenneth W. Lemke, "Asset Valuation and Income Theory," *Accounting Review* 41, no. 1 (January1966): 41.

35. Homer A. Black, *Interperiod Allocation of Corporate Income Taxes: Accounting Research Study no. 9* : (New York: AICPA, 1966): 84.

36. Robert R. Sterling, "Conservatism: The Fundamental Principle of Valuation in Traditional Accounting," *Abacus* 3, no. 2 (December 1967): 130.

37. Sybil C. Mobley, "Measures of Income," *Accounting Review* 43, no. 2 (April 1968): 338.

38. R. H. Parker, "Discounted Cash Flow in Historical Perspective," *Journal of Accounting Research* 6, no. 1 (Spring 1968): 71.

39. Paul Rosenfield, "Reporting Subjective Gains and Losses," *Accounting Review,* October 1969: 797.

40. Committee on External Reporting, American Accounting Association, "An Evaluation of External Reporting Practices, A Report of the 1966–68 Committee on External Reporting," *Accounting Review* 44, suppl. (1969): 79–123.

2
Discounting in Recent Accounting Literature

While the literature on the use of discounting in financial accounting prior to 1970 was characterized mainly by its recommendation that present values can provide useful information, starting in the mid-1960s and certainly by the 1970s, the literature became quite sophisticated. Authors began to assess more detailed and complex issues regarding the applicability of present value concepts to financial accounting.

The post-1970 academic literature on the use of discounting in financial reporting reviewed in this chapter is organized into five categories. First is the literature that deals with the general topic of the desirability of using discounting in financial accounting. Second is the literature that deals with the use of discounting in valuing assets. Third is the literature on the use of discounting in the valuation of liabilities. The fourth category is the literature that relates present value concepts to the measurement of enterprise income. The last is the literature that relates measurement attributes to discounted cash flow techniques.

Using Discounting in Financial Reporting

In 1970, Robert R. Sterling organized a symposium to bring together representatives from each major school of thought on the proper method of valuing assets and measuring income. One of the schools of thought represented at this conference advocated the use of discounted cash flows as measures of economic income. The paper that discussed this school of thought was presented by George Staubus. He hypothesized "that the property of an asset or a liability that is most frequently relevant to the decisions for which accounting data are helpful is the difference in the present value of the firm's future cash flows that will result from the existence of the asset or liability." Staubus further contended that "The most useful meaning of asset and liability quantities is the item's incremental effect upon the net discounted amount of the entity's future cash flows."[1]

R. J. Chambers, also in 1970, authored an article in which he presented a position against the use of present value in financial accounting. He argued that present values did not survey information on the magnitude of the resources available to a firm at any time and they did not indicate which of the many alternatives was financially optimum. He contended that present value accounting was essentially static, providing no informational base.[2]

In 1971, Harold Bierman, Jr. wrote an article which had several objectives, one of which was to point out the use of discounting to understand changes in value because of price level adjustments as "one example of how the concept of discounted cash flow may be used to better understand the application of accounting techniques to reporting economic events."[3] Also in 1971, R. J. Chambers wrote a review of Irving Fisher's work. He noted that some parts of Fisher's work lent support to the view that balance sheet values of assets should be market values or prices, while other parts of Fisher's work lent support to the view that balance sheet values should be present values of expected net proceeds of assets even though they might be different from market values.[4]

Lawrence Revsine authored a book in 1973, in which he discussed a normative investor model. In this model, the primacy of potential cash flow was emphasized, suggesting that investors were primarily concerned with the level and timing of future cash inflows. He concluded that, to be relevant to decision making, accounting data must provide some reasonable basis for estimating future returns and their variability.[5]

George J. Staubus, in another paper in 1973, emphasized discounted cash flow as a measurement method. He contended that a set of criteria for the usefulness of financial information should be used by accountants in choosing the best measurement method in a specific situation. Staubus took the position that discounted future cash flow data were always more relevant to cash flow oriented decisions than the data produced with any of the other less desirable methods. He contended that the discounted future cash flow method was generally the most relevant method for noncash items.[6]

In a 1974 publication, Joshua Ronen examined the feasibility of applying the discounted cash flow system to an actual firm. He attempted to provide some insight into the time and effort required for such a system and expressed the opinion that estimates of cash flows attributable to specific assets or groups of assets could be obtained at relatively little time and cost. As the review of the literature in this report indicates, others were not so sanguine and did not share Ronen's assessment of the ease of using discounting.[7]

That same year, 1974, C. J. Warrell maintained that a more satisfactory basis of valuation was needed than historical cost. In his paper, he suggested an "enterprise value concept." Warrell commented that when we consider the value of the enterprise, the appropriate figure is the expected future net receipts discounted to their present worth by probability and interest factors. But applying this approach to an individual asset confused two qualities relating to the asset: the value to the enterprise of the mere possession of the asset versus the value to the enterprise of the efficiency with which the asset is expected to be used. Warrell suggested a marginal analysis which would make the value of an asset to an enterprise equal to the decrement in the total value of the enterprise arising from the removal of that asset from the group.[8]

Concepts of discounting and present value could be found in most accounting texts and in many papers by the mid-1970s. For example, in 1975, Paul E. Dascher. V. C. Brenner, and J. J. Benjamin reviewed "the basic techniques of present value." The topic was considered important by the authors and they contended "that the present value concepts will be used by accountants to an even greater extent in the future." Frederic M. Stiner and Roger T. W. Tang co-authored a paper in 1976 that had the purpose of summarizing and commenting on the arguments relating to asset valuation methods. One valuation method addressed was discountted cash flows. They recognized the contributions of George J. Staubus in having accountants recognize the relevance of present value in valuation and in providing information of assistance in making economic decisions.[9]

A major research study, led by George M. Scott, funded by the Touche Ross Foundation and published in 1978, related to the use of present value in financial accounting. A major conclusion of this study was that current value measures were better predictors of future operating cash flows than historical cost. It was shown that investors and creditors required accounting values about individual resources and obligations to assist in their predictions of company cash flows and liquidity. A number of advantages to management of using current value measures were also indicated . Scott contended that managers would be assisted in strategic planning, managerial control, operations control, and external relations when such values were available.

This study used the INFLAN computer simulation model to examine the relationship of operating cash flows to historical cost net income and to various measures in conformance with the current value accounting model. It found that there "was strong evidence that at least one of the current value measurements examined outperforms historical cost net income as a predictor of the next year's operating cash flows in most of the wide variety of inflationary conditions simulated." The study indicated that discount rates should compensate for the time value of money, inflation expectations, and risk, and that they should also encompass the term structure of interest rates appropriate for the particular resource.

The study concluded that when present value cannot be reasonably estimated, another measurement approach should be used to establish a current cost surrogate. A significant contribution of this study was the establishment of cash flow prediction as a major purpose of financial statements.[10]

In 1977, 1978, and 1979, Joe J. Cramer published in three parts the results of his substantial research effort devoted to the use of discounting in financial accounting. Part 1 covered several topics and pointed out that a clear-cut classification of assets and liabilities into three categories—operating versus financial, monetary versus nonmonetary, and short versus long-term—helped determine the applicability of discounting. He concluded that monetary and nonmonetary items were subject to different risks. The second part of Cramer's study focused on the role of discounting in accounting for financial assets and liabilities. He concluded that discounting was equally useful for monetary and nonmonetary financial items. In the third part of his study, he indicated that, unlike financial assets, the value of operating assets was affected by all the risks and uncertainties that characterize the earnings process and, therefore, the direct discounting of such assets was of limited usefulness as an accounting measure.[11]

Two books that addressed present value in financial reporting were published in 1981. In one, William H. Beaver observed that the notion that financial statement data ought to provide useful information for the assessment of future cash flows appeared to be relatively innocuous. However, Beaver questioned this position for two reasons. First, the concept of economic income is not well defined when markets are imperfect or incomplete. Second, even in situations where markets for financial claims exist, there has been an inability to reach a consensus on the "best" method of reporting.[12]

In the other 1981 book, Ahmed Belkaoui observed that the "maintenance of productive capacity" required the use of current values for assets and liabilities. He noted that there were several methods of calculating current value: (1) present-value, (2) current entry price, (3) current exit price, and (4) a combination of values derived by the first three methods.[13]

In 1984, Diran Bodenhorn assessed what a balance sheet would look like based upon potential cash flow (service potentials) and what problems would be involved in its construction. Bodenhorn tried to prove that a useful balance sheet could be constructed based upon potential cash flow. He discussed the process and feasibility of constructing the whole balance sheet of a firm using discounted present values of expected cash flows for each asset and liability and compared the results with those under Generally Accepted Accounting Principles (GAAP), those using market values, and those under cash flow accounting. Bodenhorn concluded that using this approach would present the balance sheet in "net value" terms of each of its items, or contra values within.[14]

Vernon Kam reviewed present value in the discussion of asset and liability measurement in his 1986 book on accounting theory. He observed that present value theory has found wide acceptance because it appears that rational people in business behave in the way assumed by the theory. Thus, it appeared to him that the present value method is an ideal approach for ascertaining value.[15]

Discounting in Asset Valuation

The discussion of a number of aspects of the use of discounting in asset valuation is examined in this section. These aspects include the role of market structures, investor variations in utility functions, agency problems arising from the separation of managers from owners and creditors, the additivity of asset values, difficulties in estimating appropriate measures of expected inflation, and the assessment of relevant risks and appropriate discount rates associated with future benefits.

The Role of Market Structures

Michael Bromwich, in 1975, examined the usefulness of the net present value concept to value assets in imperfect markets such as various forms of oligopoly and monopoly. In another paper, in 1977, Bromwich considered several arguments that have been put forward for the use of net present values for asset valuation, and argued that the present value model might give investors different results depending on the structure of the market for that product. He recommended that firms focus on disclosing details regarding the "variables that underlie such present value calculations."[16]

In 1985, R. K. Ashton examined whether and under what conditions the use of replacement cost–net realizable value as bases of valuation in financial reports would provide a robust proxy of an asset's expected present value when market imperfections were present in the final goods markets. Ashton analyzed the problem from neoclassical theory and recent developments in theories of monopoly and oligopoly. His 1985 paper is an extension of the work of Michael Bromwich's in 1975, considering three market structures consistent with only normal profit. It was concluded that under certain assumptions and circumstances, the replacement–cost, (RC), net realizable value, (NRV), and the present value methods would produce close results. The author concluded that net present values will give the same results as RC–NRV only when product markets are perfectly competitive.[17]

John Cook and Oscar Holzmann, writing in 1976, examined whether replacement cost income is an ideal surrogate measure of economic income of enterprises operating in perfectly competitive markets. They observed that a necessary condition is the presence of general equality between the market prices of assets and the expected present values of their future cash flows. Unlike others (for example, Ashton, 1985), they contended that this condition may generally be expected.[18]

Investor Variations in Utility Functions

It has been argued that corporate estimates of present values of long-lived assets are inadequate for external users of financial information. For example, Michael Bromwich in 1977 contended that the present value model could serve as an ideal valuation model only under fairly restricted conditions and that a single present value estimate could not serve all investors under all circumstances. He suggested that efforts should be addressed to disclosing the fundamental variables that underlay such present value calculations versus the present values as determined by management.[19]

Separation of Managers, Owners, and Creditors

J. J. Forker, in 1984, pointed out that "within the accrual accounting framework . . . managerial estimates of PV [present value] for assets . . . that provide signals of managerial expectations about the future prospects of the firm . . . are considered unacceptable." Thus, Forker took the position that the present value method is misleading because the valuations are subjectively made by management. He contended that accountants do not have the competence to establish the values of the assets of a going concern.[20]

Additivity of Asset Values

A number of authors have considered the desirability of adding up the values of individual assets to obtain the value of the going concern. For example, because of correlations among the cash flows for different assets, adding up the individual asset values will rarely result in a number equal to the value of the whole firm.[21]

In a 1973 paper, Richard Brief and Joel Owen illustrated the use of the internal rate of return for valuing a firm with many assets, by examining both the multi-asset problem and revenue separability according to estimation theory.

The authors concluded that the internal rate of return is a firm-wide approach and not an appropriate single-asset model. This view was not widely accepted; subsequent commentators claimed that Brief and Owen's conclusion was not valid and was misleading. Brief and Owen replied that the basic issue in their paper was the problem of interpreting aggregated present value data for the firm.[22]

In addition to applying the discounted cash flow system to an actual firm in 1974, Ronen presented a conceptual approach to discounted cash flow accounting. He observed that the individual present values assigned to assets and liabilities would not necessarily add up to the total present value of the firm. In addition, he noted that there existed two quantifications of expected cash flows—the cash flow expected by the firm's management and the cash flow expected by others.[23]

Similarly, in a 1984 book on accounting theory, Harry I. Wolk, Jere R. Francis, and Michael G. Tearney pointed out that one problem with the application of discounted cash flows was that many assets contribute jointly to the production of cash flows. Another problem was the formidable estimation problem of future cash flows. The authors concluded that discounted cash flow could be applied to only a very restricted group of assets and liabilities when interest and principal payments were directly stipulated or could be imputed.[24]

Vernon Kam observed that the present value approach could be used for financial reporting purposes but that its use was limited because, the future cash flows from most non-monetary assets, are difficult to ascertain. While the net cash receipts of a firm are generated by all its assets, it would be arbitrary to allocate certain amounts to each fixed asset.[25]

Richard G. Schroeder, Levis D. McCullers, and Myrtle Clark were co-authors of a 1987 book on accounting theory that commented on measurement techniques used in financial reporting. They felt that, because of the different measurement techniques used, a summation of assets on the typical balance sheet was much like adding apples and oranges. In their opinion, a presentation of information about the expected future benefits would be more appropriate.[26]

Estimation of Expected Inflation

In 1971, Harold Bierman, Jr. provided formulae for discounting when there were price level adjustments and cautioned that applying price level adjustments to values based upon net present values (NPVs) would lead to double counting because the discount rate calculations used in NPV already includes expected rates of inflation .[27]

Difficulty in Assessing Relevant Risks and Rates

Kenneth S. Most authored an accounting theory book in 1977 that included frequent comments on the theory of using present value in financial accounting. He recognized the early contributions of Irving Fisher and John Canning and observed that Fisher recognized the discount factor as being the marginal rate at which society will substitute future satisfactions for present satisfactions. While it was traditionally believed that the equivalent concept for a firm was the cost of capital, he commented that the current prevailing view was that the appropriate discount rate is a risk-adjusted rate of interest.[28]

Ahmed Belkaoui observed that most authors define the discount rate as the subjective rate of return, but that several appropriate discount rates may be used to compute capitalized value: (1) the historical rate of discount, (2) the current rate of discount, (3) the average expected rate of discount, (4) the weighted average cost of capital, and (5) the incremental borrowing rate.[29]

C. Torben Thomsen, in 1984, discussed the temporal distortions induced by discounting. He made the point that, by understanding time distortions introduced by discounting, the user of present value calculations could guard against using discounting where it was not warranted. When discount rates are high, the time horizon became biased toward the near term-future. Thomsen contended that it was unrealistic to assume that high interest rates (discount rates) could continue over an extended period of time. He indicated that the use of a given discount rate implied that the risk of future cash flows increased exponentially and that the associated present value decreased exponentially. This temporal pattern of risk may not be consistent with reality.[30]

Measurement Attributes of Net Present Values

One of the objectives of Harold Bierman, Jr's. 1971 paper was to give an example of how the concept of discounted cash flow might be used to better understand the use of accounting techniques in reporting economic events while discussing accounting for long-lived assets during periods of changing price levels. Thomas R. Dyckman and Willis R. Greer commented critically on the article in separate papers. Bierman replied that there were no errors in his article, but that there were opportunities for extension, and he acknowledged that Dyckman and Greer extended the model. Russell J. Peterson and Thomas F. Keller further extended Bierman's analysis in their paper, "Asset Valuation, Income Determination and Changing Prices."[31]

Amir Barnea and Harold Bierman, Jr. considered three alternative concepts of asset valuation in 1974: replacement cost, present value, and resale value. They maintained that all three measures have relevance, but that it was useful to report separately the value of an asset to a specific firm versus market measures of that value.[32]

Michael Bromwich, in 1975, maintained that present value, as the valuation system in financial accounting, was normally impractical. The present value model was, therefore, relegated to aiding in the selection of more practical valuation systems, such as replacement cost or net realizable value. He concluded that neither replacement cost nor net realizable value are reliable surrogates for present value.[33]

In 1985, Carl J. Norstrom indicated that the accounting literature often used three alternative general bases for the value of an asset: the replacement cost of the asset, the net realizable value of the asset, and the present value of the expected future net receipts from the asset. The purpose of this paper was to provide a reasonably unified treatment of value under conditions of certainty when the purchase price of the asset is higher than its net realizable value. Norstrom used two numerical illustrations. In one, he showed that it might be best to reinvest even when the present value of an existing asset was less than the purchase price of another asset of that age. In the other illustration, he showed that it might be best not to reinvest in new assets even though the present value exceeded the purchase price.[34]

George Staubus published a major paper on measurement in 1985, in which he presented a descriptive theory of accounting measurement. Among other things, he examined specific measurement practices to ascertain what measurement methods were used and the qualities characterizing those methods. Staubus identified eight basic measurement methods in current use: current market price, future cash flows, present value of future cash flows, net realizable value, original proceeds, and equity. He concluded that the present value of future cash flows was the most acceptable accounting principle.[35]

Frequency of Updating Present Values

In a 1987 paper, Walter Schuetze reviewed problems in current practice on when to recognize "impairment" of long-lived nonmonetary assets. One of the practical problems was how write-downs to recognize impairments should be measured. Should discounted future cash flows be used? If discounted future cash flows are to be used, what should be the discount rate?[36]

Capitalization of Financing Costs

The topic of whether some interest cost should be capitalized has been the subject of considerable discussion in accounting literature. Some maintain that interest on borrowed funds should be capitalized when the related assets are not yet earning revenues, such as construction work in progress. Some also maintain that part of the cost of certain nonearning assets should include interest on funds attributable to stockholders' equity. In his 1943 *Accountants Handbook*, William A. Paton discusses the relationship between capitalized interest and present value depreciation. *Statement of Financial Accounting Standard No. 34* provides for the capitalization of interest on borrowed funds when the related assets are not yet earning revenues. Only special industries such as the public utility industry are allowed to include interest on funds attributable to stockholders' equity.[37]

In a 1982 article entitled "Equity Interest: Its Time Has Come," Robert Anthony proposes to capitalize the cost of equity financing and the cost of interest for plant and equipment during construction and for inventory and other current assets while they are held.[38] The issue of capitalizing interest may be outside the scope of discounting interest. Capitalizing interest can be viewed as an issue of what is the proper cost to be added to an asset versus expensing such a cost. The issue of discounting relates to future flows being discounted to the present.

Discounting in the Valuation of Liabilities

Cecil Dollar, Jr. contended, in 1973, that liabilities should be valued at current values when assets are also measured at current values. However, since assets are usually carried at cost, liabilities are for the most part being measured correctly.[39]

In a 1983 paper, Carrick A. Martin observed that the idea has been promoted by several writers that long-term liabilities should be reported at their current market values. In this paper, Martin took the opposite view—that incorporation of current yields on liabilities would produce misleading information. Martin made the case that reporting current market values of liabilities would be misleading with respect to operating performance, financial stability, and capital maintenance.[40]

Also in1983, Donald S. Shannon and William Stevens commented that bonds are recorded initially at their present value and that any initial premium or discount recorded is amortized over the life of the bond issue. Subsequent to the date of issue, changes in the market value of the bond are not recognized and, therefore, "economic reality" is not recognized. Upon early extinguishment of the debt, therefore, the accumulated gain or loss is recognized as extraordinary because the bond was not adjusted to economic reality during its life. In this article they took the position that a more relevant method needs to be used, one that recognizes economic reality during the life of the bond. This method would improve financial reporting and remove a serious motivational conflict from management when an early extinguishment of the debt decision is made.[41]

Fred A. Jacobs, Larry H. Beard, and Al L. Hartgraves agreed that there is a need for current value information about long-term debt. If long-term debt is undervalued or overvalued, the analysis of a financial statement could be distorted. They demonstrated revaluation of long-term debt using present value calculations and showed the effect of this revaluation on capital position rates.[42]

Richard G. Schroeder, Levis D. McCullers, and Myrtle Clark were co-authors of a 1987 accounting theory book in which they noted that current liabilities are usually measured at their liquidation value, ignoring the time value of money, that long-term liabilities are frequently measured at present value using the yield rate at the date of issue, and that valuations of liability are not changed to reflect changes in the market rates of interest.[43]

Discounting and Measurement of Income

Robert R. Sterling was the author of a book in 1970 that reviewed the theory underlying the measurement of income. He concluded that the problem was not with the definition of income but with the application of the concept of income. He noted that one of the approaches to the measurement of income came from Irving Fisher and that it was stated best by Edwards and Bell as follows:

> In the absence of dividend payments and new contributions by stockholders, income is measured at the end of the period by adding up the discounted values of all net receipts which the managers then expect to earn on the firm's existing net assets and subtracting from this subjective value a similar computation made at the beginning of the period.[44]

Sterling indicated that the usual criticism of this concept was based on subjectivity and future uncertainty.

In 1975, T. A. Lee reviewed the fundamental relationship between income and capital. Lee pointed out that in accounting, capital and income were regarded as a stock and a flow, respectively. The stocks (the balance sheet) result from transacted flows which are accounted for when measuring accounting income. The stock-flow dichotomy also exists in economics through the valuation of capital as a discounted future stream of income, income being the expired portion of capital.[45]

Ahmed Belkaoui noted that the present-value concept of income is based upon estimates of income expected to be accrued within the firm's planning horizon. These estimates of future income could be computed when the relevant variables are known or when the probabilities of all of the relevant variables could be estimated.[46]

Along with most finance academics, Joel Stern stressed an economic model that held "that the market value of corporate stock is the present value of a company's future expected after-tax free cash flows, discounted at rates which reflect investors' required returns for bearing risk. . . . When earnings seriously misrepresent operating cash flows, accounting statements distort performance and provide an unreliable guide to value."[47]

Discounting and Goals for Accounting Measurement

In a 1970 paper, Richard Mattessich maintained that the accounting system has to serve management as well as legalistic objectives, and that a dualistic or even multidimensional valuation is desirable and often indispensable. Thus, he contended, the controversy was not around the issue of whether assets should or should not be valued at present value or other values, but about whether these values should systematically be incorporated into the accounting information system.[48]

R. J. Chambers took issue with Mattessich. According to Chambers, present values are necessary in decision making, as are other measurements. He maintained that because all measurements are not the same, only confusion could result from using different measurements. Mattessich and Chambers elaborated on their respective positions in the March–April 1971 and July–August 1971 issues of *Cost and Management*.[49]

In 1977, Edward J. McIntyre commented that present value depreciation had been explored in the literature as a means of reconciling the conflict between the use the of the internal rate of return in capital budgeting versus the accounting return on investment computed from financial statement data. He concluded that there are various accounting methods that provide compatibility between the two, but that they might yield individual account balances which lack economic substance.[50]

K. V. Peasnell recognized, in 1977, that the discounted present value concept played an important role in accounting theory. However, there were those who argued that the primary function of financial accounting is the assessment of achievements, which indicates a need for ex post facto measures. He argued that accountants do not have a comparative advantage in the determination of discounted present value for investors and that this task should be left to the stock market.[51]

In 1978, Laurence A. Friedman discussed some of the major valuation techniques which could be considered for providing measures of current value. These included replacement cost, exit value, and discounted cash flows, all of which could be general price-level adjusted. Friedman noted that many experts considered determining projected future cash flows and the appropriate discount rate to be a completely subjective exercise.[52]

Also in1978, A. T. Craswell noted that surrogates were used in accounting behavioral research and in accounting theory. He contended that "outside of the perfect market, present values exist only in the minds of individuals and, therefore, are incorrigible." He indicated that various surrogates had been proposed and argued that these various valuation bases could not, in general, be substituted for present values and justified as surrogates. Conceptually, historical cost, replacement cost, net realizable value, and present value are separate, may give rise to differences in valuation and therefore could not be interchanged in accounting theories.[53]

In a 1984 accounting theory book, Harry I. Wolk, Jere R. Francis, and Michael G. Tearney discussed discounted cash flows under current value systems. The authors did not favor using discounted cash flows as a valuation system. They regarded it as a theoretical method with virtually no operable practicability for financial statements. They indicated that with discounted cash flows, both asset valuation and income measurement are anchored to future expectations.[54]

Conclusions

The post-1970s academic literature on discounting in financial reporting was found to be more extensive and generally more sophisticated and complex than the discussions of this topic prior to the 1970s. The use of discounting concepts in financial accounting was becoming widely accepted in the 1970s and the 1980s.

Notes

1. George J. Staubus, "The Relevance of Evidence of Cash Flows," *Asset Valuation and Income Determination,* edited by Robert R. Sterling (Lawrence, Kans.: Scholars Book Co., 1970): 48, 50.

2. R. J. Chambers, "Present Value Accounting," *Accountant*, April 16, 1970: 555.
3. Harold Bierman, Jr., "Discounted Cash Flows, Price Level Adjustments and Expectations," *Accounting Review* 46, no. 4 (October 1971): 693.
4. R. J. Chambers, "Income and Capital: Fisher's Legacy," *Journal of Accounting Research* 9, no. 1 (Spring 1971): 137–49.
5. Lawrence Revsine, *Replacement Cost Accounting* (Englewood Cliffs, N.J.: Prentice-Hall, 1973).
6. George J. Staubus, "The Measurement of Assets and Liabilities," *Accounting & Business Research*, no. 3 (Autumn 1973): 243–62.
7. Joshua Ronen, "A Test of the Feasibility of Preparing Discounted Cash Flow Accounting Statements," *AICPA Objectives of Financial Statements,* 2 May 1974, 202–12.
8. C. J. Warrell, "The Enterprise Value Concept of Asset Valuation," *Accounting & Business Research*, no. 2 (Summer 1974): 220-26.
9. Paul E. Dascher, V. C. Brenner, and J. J. Benjamin, "Present Value: A Review," *National Public Accountant* 20 (June 1975): 18-21; Frederic M. Stiner and Roger Y. W. Tang, "The Controversy over Asset Valuation," *The National Public Accountant* 21 (October 1976): 26-29.
10. George M. Scott, *Research Study on Current-Value Accounting Measurements and Utility* (New York: Touche Ross Foundation 1978): 5.
11. Joe J. Cramer, "The Nature and Importance of Discounted Present Value in Financial Accounting and Reporting: Part I," *Arthur Andersen Chronicle* 37, no. 2 (September 1977): 27–37; "The Nature and Importance of Discounted Present Value in Financial Accounting and Reporting: Part I," *Arthur Andersen Chronicle* 38, no. 1 (June 1978): 46–56; "The Nature and Importance of Discounted Present Value in Financial Accounting and Reporting: Part III," *Arthur Andersen Chronicle* 39, no. 1 (June 1979): 43–48.
12. William H. Beaver, *Financial Reporting: An Accounting Revolution* (Englewood Cliffs, N.J.: Prentice-Hall, 1981).
13. Ahmed Belkaoui, *Accounting Theory* (New York: Harcourt Brace Jovanovich, 1981), 147.
14. Diran Bodenhorn, "Balance Sheet Items as the Present Value of Future Cash Flows," *Journal of Business, Finance, & Accounting* 11, no. 4 (Winter 1984): 493–510.

15. Vernon Kam, *Accounting Theory* (New York: Wiley,1986).
16. Michael Bromwich, "Asset Valuation with Imperfect Markets," *Accounting & Business Research*, no. 3 (Autumn 1975): 242–53, idem, "The Use of Present Value Valuation Models in Published Accounting Reports," *Accounting Review* 52, no. 3 (July 1977): 587–95.
17. R. K. Ashton, "Asset Valuation and Imperfect Markets: An Extension," *Accounting & Business Research* no. 1 (Spring 1985): 123–27.
18. John S. Cook and Oscar J. Holzmann, "Current Cost and Present Value in Income Theory," *Accounting Review* 51, no. 4 (October 1976): 778–87.
19. Bromwich, "Use of Present Value Valuation Models."
20. J. J. Forker, "Contract Value Accounting and the Monitoring of Managerial Performance: An Agency-Based Proposal," *Accounting & Business Research*, no. 1 (Spring 1984): 125–37.
21. Joshua Ronen, "Discounted Cash Flow Accounting," *AICPA Objectives of Financial Statements,* 1974, 143–60.
22. Richard Brief and Joel Owen, "Present Value Models and the Multi-Asset Problem," *Accounting Review* 48, no. 4 (October 1973): 690–95; Stephen L. Meyers, "Present Value Models and the Multi- Asset Problem: A Comment," *Accounting Review* 48, no. 4 (October 1973): 816–18; Anthony Curley and Charles G. Carpenter, "Present Value Models and the Multi-Asset Problem: Comment," *Accounting Review* 48, no. 4 (October 1973): 812–15; Richard Brief and Joel Owen, "Present Value Models and the Multi-Asset Problem: A Reply", *Accounting Review* 48, no. 4 (October 1973): 819–21.
23. Ronen, "Test of Feasibility."
24. Harry I. Wolk, Jere R. Francis, and Michael G. Tearney, *Accounting Theory*, (Boston: Kent Publishing, 1984).
25. Kam, *Accounting Theory.*
26. Richard G. Schroeder, Levis D. McCullers, and Myrtle Clark, *Accounting Theory* (New York: Wiley, 1987), 188–91.
27. Harold Bierman, Jr., "Discounted Cash Flows, Price Level Adjustments and Expectations," *Accounting Review* 46, no. 4 (October 1971): 693–99.
28. Kenneth S. Most, *Accounting Theory* (Columbus: Grid, 1977).
29. Belkaoui, *Accounting Theory.*

30. C. Torben Thomsen, "Dangers in Discounting," *Management Accounting*, January 1984, 37–39.

31. Bierman, "Discounted Cash Flows"; Thomas R. Dyckman, "Discounted Cash Flows, Price-Level Adjustments and Expectations: A Comment," *Accounting Review* 47, no. 4 (October 1972): 794–98, Willis R. Greer, Jr., "Discounted Cash Flows, Price-Level Adjustments and Expectations: A Comment," *Accounting Review* 47, no. 3 (July 1972): 587–88, Harold Bierman, Jr., "Discounted Cash Flows, Price Level Adjustments and Expectations: A Reply," *Accounting Review* 47, no. 3 (July 1972): 589–90 and *Accounting Review* 47, no. 4 (October 1972): 788–99, Russell J. Peterson and Thomas F. Keller, "Asset Valuation, Income Determination and Changing Prices," *Accounting Review* 47, no. 4 (October 1972): 801–5.

32. Amir Barnea and Harold Bierman, Jr., "Cash Flow Valuation and Depreciation," *Accounting and Business Research*, no. 2 (Summer 1974): 193–96.

33. Michael Bromwich, "Asset Valuation."

34. Carl J. Norstrom, "The Deprival Value of Durable Assets," *Accounting and Business Research*, no. 3 (Autumn 1985): 265–70.

35. George J. Staubus, "An Induced Theory of Accounting Measurement," *Accounting Review* 60, no. 1 (January 1985): 53–75.

36. Walter Schuetze, "Disclosure and the Impairment Question," *Journal of Accountancy*, December 1987, 26–32.

37. William A. Paton, *Accountant's Handbook*, 3d ed. (New York: Ronald Press, 1943); Financial Accounting Standards Board (FASB), *Statement of Financial Accounting Standard*, no. 34: *Capitalization of Interest Cost* (Stamford, Conn.: FASB, 1980).

38. Robert Anthony, "Equity Interest: Its Time Has Come," *Journal of Accountancy*, December 1982.

39. Cecil Dollar, Jr., "Measurement of Liabilities at Current Values," *National Public Accountant* 18, (January 1973): 24–25.

40. Carrick A. Martin, "The Current Cost of a Quoted Long-Term Liability," *Accounting and Business Research*, no. 2 (Summer 1983): 191–99.

41. Donald S. Shannon and William Stevens, "How Debt Refunding Can Cause Decision Conflicts," *Management Accounting*, December 1983, 40–44.

42. Fred A. Jacobs, Larry H. Beard, and Al L. Hartgraves, "Distortion of Financial Statements: Inflation's Impact on Long-Term Debt," *Credit and Financial Management,* February 1983, 15–33.

43. Schroeder, McCullers, and Clark, *Accounting Theory,* 188–191.

44. Robert R. Sterling, *Theory of the Measurement of Enterprise Income* (Lawrence, Kans.: University Press of Kansas, 1970): 12.

45. T. A. Lee, *Income and Value Measurement: Theory and Practice* (Baltimore: University Park Press, 1975).

46. Belkaoui, *Accounting Theory*.

47. Donald H. Chew, *Six Roundtable Discussions of Corporate Finance with Joel Stern* (New York: Quorum Books, 1986).

48. Richard Mattessich, "On the Perennial Misunderstanding of Asset Measurement by Means of Present Value," *Cost and Management,* March–April 1970, 30.

49. R. J. Chambers, "Asset Measurement and Valuation," *Cost and Management,* March–April 1971, 30–35; Richard Mattessich, "On Further Misunderstandings about Asset Measurement and Valuation: A Rejoinder to Chambers' Article," *Cost and Management,* March–April 1971: 36–42; R. J. Chambers, "Measurement and Valuation Again," *Cost and Management,* July–August 1971: 12–17; Richard Mattessich, "Asset Measurement and Valuation: A Final Reply to Chambers," *Cost and Management,* July–August 1971: 18–23.

50. Edward V. McIntyre, "Present Value Depreciation and the Disaggregation Problem," *Accounting Review,* 52, no. 1 (January 1977):162–71.

51. K. V. Peasnell, "A Note on the Discounted Present Value Concept," *Accounting Review* 52, no. 1, (January 1977): 186–89.

52. Laurence A. Friedman, "What is Current Value?" *CPA Journal,* November 1978, 24–28.

53. A. T. Craswell, "Surrogates in Accounting," *Abacus* 14, (June 1978): 81–93.

54. Wolk, Francis, and Tearney, *Accounting Theory.*

3

Discounting Included in Guidance to the Setting of Standards

There have been a number of attempts to provide guidance to the process of setting standards. In general, these attempts could be described as a deductive approach to standard setting: in other words, they provide objectives to guide the standard setting process.

These studies and reports have consistently recognized a role for the use of present value in financial reporting. They are reviewed here with regard to their discussion of the use of discounting and cash flow assessments.

Early Guidance to Standard Setting

The American Institute of Accountants published *Statement of Accounting Principles* in 1938, a study authored by Thomas H. Sanders, Henry R. Hatfield, and U. Moore. In this statement, the following reference is made to accounting for bond discount.

> . . . the discount is in a sense an offset to the liability from which it arises, having the mathematical effect of reducing that liability to its present worth. But the practice is well established of showing the bond liability at its face value. When, therefore, the bonds are issued at a discount, a contra item is involved.[1]

This is a significant early guide to the use of present value in financial reporting.

In, 1957, the American Accounting Association published its committee report, *Accounting and Reporting Standards for Corporate Financial Statements and Preceding Statements and Supplements*, almost twenty years after the first guide to standards setting discussed above. This American Accounting Association committee's report suggests that present worth is the ideal guide to the measurement of an asset:

> The value of an asset is the money-equivalent of its service potentials. Conceptually, this is the sum of the future market prices of all streams of service to be derived, discounted by probability and interest factors to their present worth. However, the conception of value is an abstraction which yields but limited practical basis for quantification. Consequently, the measurement of assets is commonly made by other more feasible methods.
>
> Monetary assets—cash or claims to cash—should be expressed in terms of expected cash receipts adjusted for collection delay where significant. Cash on hand, demand deposits, and short-term government receivables are readily expressed in such terms because the force of interest and the uncertainty of collection are negligible. Other claims to cash may require adjustment to measure current realizable amounts. Accounts or notes receivable should be discounted for stated or implied interest factors; if material, they should also be reduced by allowances to cover shrinkage on collection. Still other cash claims may involve equitable consideration, as in the measurement of receivables arising from long-term construction contracts on a percentage of completion basis. In every case, however, the amount of monetary assets should be based on discernible, measurable, and reasonably certain collection and availability of cash."[2]

The Special Committee on Research Program of the American Institute of Certified Public Accountants (AICPA) proposed a study of the basic postulates underlying accounting and a study of the broad principles of accounting. The studies were intended to serve as the foundation for the entire body of future pronouncements by the Accounting Principles Board (APB) of the AICPA.

The first of these studies, authored in 1961 by Maurice Moonitz, *The Basic Postulates of Accounting: Accounting Research Study, No. 1*, does not refer directly to the use of present value in financial reporting. The companion study, by Robert Sprouse and Maurice Moonitz in 1962, *A Tentative Set of Broad Accounting principles For Business Enterprises: Accounting Research Study, [ARS] no 3*, does include the use of present value in financial reporting. Chapter 4 of this study describes the use of present value for money or claims to money:

> As a general rule, the valuation of these assets should be based on the amount of cash into which they will be converted, that is, their discounted future exchange prices. Cash itself, whether represented by bank deposits or coins and currency, is measured by count and summation. Domestic holdings are then valued at their face amount; convertible foreign holdings are translated into the domestic equivalent.
>
> Receivables (accounts, notes, loans, advances) generally constitute monetary assets whose value is measured ideally by the present (discounted) value of the

future cash receipts to be derived from them. For the sake of accuracy, a rate of interest (discount) should be explicitly employed in calculating the present value of long-term receivables. The use of the market (effective) rate in force at the date the receivable was acquired will result in a recognition of the amount and rate of interest actually being earned by the company under the contract entered into. In the case of the short-term receivables, the period of time until collection is typically so short that the force of interest (at the rates that have prevailed in this country in recent years) may be ignored. Accordingly, short-term receivables are usually measured by the net amount expected to be collected, after making allowance for uncollectibles, cash discounts, etc.

Investments in marketable securities having known maturity values and dates and held as a secondary cash reserve may be valued along such similar lines, but since they may be converted into cash momentarily their current market price is usually more significant as a measure of their worth to the enterprise."[3]

Chapter 5 describes the use of present value for the measurement of liabilities:

From the standpoint of measurement, two broad types of liabilities can be distinguished. The one type calls for settlement in cash; the other type calls for settlement in a form other than cash.

The amounts of those obligations calling for settlement in cash should be measured by the future payments, discounted to the present by the use of a market (yield, effective) rate of interest. Where short-term obligations explicitly recognize the element of interest, as in the case of certain promissory notes, that factor should be recognized in the measurement of the liability. Where the short-term obligations do not explicitly recognize the element of interest, as in the case of trade accounts payable, the force of interest is ordinarily negligible because the span between the future payments and the present measurement is short.

In the case of long-term liabilities, the force of interest is significant and should be recognized. Hence, in the case of long-term debt, the liability is properly measured by the present (discounted) value of all future payments to be made under the contract. These future payments include periodic "interest" payments and all "principal" payments, whether in installments or in a lump sum of maturity. Ordinarily the pertinent rate of interest for determining present value is the yield rate of interest at the date of issue (also called the effective rate or market rate), which may differ from the nominal or coupon rate in the contract itself.

Where the resultant present value differs from the amount due at maturity, the

> amount of the liability is measured by deducting the amount of the "discount" from the maturity payment or adding the amount of the "premium" to the maturity payment. A "discount" does not represent an embodiment of future economic benefits and accordingly cannot constitute an asset. A "premium" has no characteristic which differentiates it from any other part of the liability. It represents an integral part of the amount received (borrowed) in exchange for a contract to make future payments, and is repaid as the provisions of the contract are complied with.[4]

Accounting Research Studies, nos. 1 and *3* were not well received by the accounting profession. Many thought them too theoretical. The AICPA decided to issue an inventory of generally accepted accounting principles to summarize the current set of standards. The *Inventory of Generally Accepted Accounting Principles: ARS, no. 7*, by Paul Grady, was issued in 1965. It is concerned with the concepts related to principles and practices which had general acceptance in 1965. Two areas that used present value were identified:

> Disclose rental charges under material leases and capitalize those which are in effect installment purchases of fixed assets.
>
> The effective rate of interest that will prevail in the bond market cannot be estimated precisely prior to issuing the bonds. A difference between the nominal rate of interest (i.e., the rate the issuer agrees to pay on the face amount of the bond issue) and the effective rate results in the bonds being issued at either a premium or discount depending on which rate is higher. The bonds-payable account is usually credited for the face amount and the premium or discount is charged or credited to a separate account, the amount of which is amortized over the life of the bond issue.[5]

The AICPA also issued the APB's *Statement no. 4: Basic Concepts and Accounting Principles Underlying Financial Statements of Business Enterprises*, in 1970. The purpose of the *Statement* was to provide a basis for guiding the future development of financial accounting. In several areas, the present value concept was used. Paragraph 70 included a comment that four types of money prices are used in measuring resources in financial accounting. One was:

> . . . price based on future exchanges. . . . This price is used in several related concepts—present value of future net money receipts, discounted cash flow, (discounted) net realizable value, and value in use. Each indicates that the amount ascribed to the resource is measured by the expected net future money flow related to the resource in its present or expected use by the enterprise, discounted for an interest factor.

Paragraph 181 covered the principles to guide the selection of events and assignment of dollar amounts. Several comments that related to present value:

> M-1A. Acquisition cost of assets. Assets acquired in exchanges are measured at the exchange price, that is, at acquisition cost. Money and money claims acquired are measured at their face amount or sometimes at their discounted amount. Discussion. Cash, accounts receivable, and other short-term money claims are usually measured at their face amount. A long-term non-interest bearing note receivable is measured at its discounted amount. . . .
>
> M-1C. Amount of liabilities. Liabilities are measured at amounts established in the exchanges, usually the amounts to be paid, sometimes discounted. Discussion. Conceptually, a liability is incurred. Most short-term liabilities are simply measured at the amount to be paid. Discounted present values are often used if the obligations require payments at dates that are relatively far in the future. Pension obligations and liabilities under capitalized long-term leases are measured at discounted amounts. Bonds and other long-term liabilities are in effect measured at the discounted amount of the future cash payments for interest and principal. The difference between the recorded amount of a liability and the amounts to be paid is amortized over the periods to maturity.[6]

In 1973, the AICPA issued a report of another study group, *Objectives of Financial Statements*. This study group was organized to seek goals that related to the information presented in financial statements. It concluded that the development of objectives should be based on the needs of external users of financial information. The study group also concluded that the objectives of financial statements could not be served by the exclusive use of a single valuation basis and identified four: historical cost, exit values, current replacement cost, and discounted cash flows.

The group recommended that valuation bases should be arrived at after giving appropriate consideration to the financial statement objectives and indicated several informational requirements:

1. Actual sacrifice for assets—actual benefits of liabilities.
2. Potential benefit of assets—potential sacrifice for liabilities.
3. Measurement of completed cycles and recognizable progress toward the completion of cycles.
4. Measurement of value changes that provided the best current indication of the outcome of incomplete cycles.[7]

Recent Guidance to Standard Setting

The Financial Accounting Standards Board initiated a project in 1973 to develop a conceptual framework for financial accounting and reporting. A 1976 *Discussion Memorandum (DM)* was developed for this project titled *An Analysis Related to the Conceptual Framework for Financial Accounting and Reporting: Elements of Financial Statements and Their Measurement.* Part 3 of the *DM* dealt with the measurement of the elements of financial statements.[8]

In this *DM*, five attributes that have been used or proposed for measuring and presenting various classes of assets and liabilities were identified and discussed. These attributes were:

1. *Historical cost–historical proceeds*—the amount paid to acquire an asset (less subsequent amortization) or the amount received when a liability was incurred.
2. *Current cost–current proceeds*—the amount required currently to obtain the same asset or the amount that would be received if the same obligation were incurred currently.
3. *Current exit value* in orderly liquidation—the amount of cash that could be obtained currently by selling an asset (that is, current market value, if a market exists), or the amount required to eliminate an obligation.
4. *Expected exit value* in due course of business—the nondiscounted amount of cash into which an asset is expected to be converted (that is, its net realizable value) or the nondiscounted amount of cash expected to be paid to eliminate a liability.
5. *Present value* of expected cash flows—the discounted amount of net cash inflows pertaining to an asset or the discounted amount of net cash outflows required to eliminate a liability.[9]

Part 3 of the *DM* also examined in some detail how each of these attributes might be applied to several major classes of assets and liabilities. It was noted that "measuring the net present value of individual assets is generally conceded to be not feasible if the future cash flows resulting from holding and utilizing the asset are unknown, not reasonably predictable, or inextricably combined with the cash flows stemming from other factors."[10]

In measuring the present value of expected cash flows, several possible appropriate rates of discount were identified:

1. *Historical rate*—The historical rate of discount is the rate of return that is implicit in the amount of cash (or other consideration) paid to acquire an asset.
2. *Current rate*—The current rate of discount is the rate of return that is implicit in the amount of cash (or other consideration) that would have to be paid if the same asset were acquired currently.
3. *Average expected rate*—The average expected rate of discount is the average rate of return that is expected to be earned on similar assets during some, usually long-term, future period.
4. *Weighted average cost of capital*—The weighted average cost of capital is based on a particular capital structure, that is, a particular ratio of long-term debt, preferred stockholders' equity, and common stockholders' equity.
5. *Incremental borrowing rate*—The incremental borrowing rate is the rate of interest that would have to be paid to obtain additional borrowed capital currently.[11]

The *DM* illustrated the similarities and differences in using historical rates and current rates with an example based on the following facts:

1. On December 31, 19X1 the enterprise acquired at face value a $5,000, 10 percent note receivable due in four years with annual interest payments to be received each December 31, and
2. One year later, on December 31, 19X2 prevailing interest rates for similar receivables had increased to 14 percent.

If, at December 31, 19X2, the receivable is measured using the interest rate that was implicit in the December 31, 19X1 transaction, that is, using the historical 10 percent interest rate, its present value would be $5,000 at December 31, 19X2. On the other hand, if at December 31, 19X2, the receivable is measured using the interest rate currently applicable to similar receivables—that is, using the current 14 percent interest rate—its present value would be $4,536 at that date.

$5,000 10 Percent Note Receivable Due December 31, 19X5
Present Value December 31, 19X2

	10%	14%
Present value of $5,000 maturity payment due December 31, 19X5		
@ 10% ($5,000 x .751)	$3,755	
@ 14% ($5,000 x .675)		$3,375
Present value of $500 interest payments due at end of each year for three years		
@ 10% ($500 x 2.487)	1,245	
@ 14% ($500 x 2.322)		1,161
	$5,000	$4,536

The use of current rates complicates the segregation of interest income from the gains or losses in present values. Theoretically, when using current rates, present values based on the current rate, and the related interest income and holding gains and losses, should be computed continuously. The aggregate return on the receivable during the entire holding period is the same whether the historical rate or current rates are used in periodic measures.[12] The *DM* presented an illustration showing alternative computations of interest income and holding gains or losses based on the current rate. That illustration is reproduced in this chapter as exhibit 3-1.

Another example in this *DM* dealt with the purchase of a long-term debt security. If this security is purchased at par, then the historical cost is identical to the measure of the present value of its future interest and maturity payments discounted at the stated interest rate. This was demonstrated in the first part of the *DM's* illustration 2, reproduced here as exhibit 3-2.

When a long-term debt security is purchased at a discount or premium, then the purchase price represents the present value of its future interest and maturity payments discounted at the effective rate of interest. As illustrated by the second part of exhibit 3-2, subsequent to the date of purchase:

> . . . the measurement of present value at the historical effective rate of interest continues to give identical results as the measurement of historical cost (more properly, historical cost adjusted for amortization of the premium or discount), provided the "interest" method of amortizing the premium or discount is used. . . . If straight-line amortization of the premium or discount were used, historical cost adjusted for amortization would differ from present value at the historical effective rate of interest but not necessarily materially."[13]

EXHIBIT 3–1 **Alternative Computations of Interest Income and Holding Gains (Losses) Based on the Current Rate**

1. Computation based on the assumption that the Interest rate changed at the beginning of the period.		*2. Computation based on the assumption that the Interest rate changed at the end of the period.*		*3. An average rate of interest during the period is determined. Computation based on the assumption that the rate changed to that average at the beginning of the period and from that average at the end of the period.**	
Present value @ 10% at January 1, 19X2	$5,000	Present value @ 10% at January 1, 19X2	$5,000	Present value @ 10% at January 1, 19X2	$5,000
Present value @ 14% at January 1, 19X2	4,417			Present value @ 11% at January 1, 19X2	4,845
Holding loss (at beginning of period)	$ 583			Holding loss (at beginning of period)	$ 155
Interest income during 19X2 ($4,417 x .14)	$ 619	Interest income during 19X2 ($5,000 x .10)	$ 500	Interest income during 19X2 ($4,845 x .11)	$ 533
Present value @ 14% at December 31, 19X2	$4,536	Present value @ 10% at December 31, 19X2	$5,000	Present value @ 11% at December 31, 19X2	$4,878
		Present value @ 14% at December 31, 19X2	4,536	Present value @ 14% at December 31, 19X2	4,536
		Holding loss (at end of period)	$ 464	Holding loss (at end of period)	$ 342

*Other assumptions about the average rate could be made. For example, it could be assumed that the rate changed *to* the average at the midpoint of the period and changed *from* the average at the end of the period.

In this illustration, the 11% average current rate for the year was based on determinations made at the end of each quarter, as follows:

EXHIBIT 3–1 *(continued)*

19X2	*current rate*	*average for quarter (beginning + ending)/2*
January 1	10%	
March 31	11%	10.5%
June 30	10%	10.5%
September 30	11%	10.5%
December 31	14%	12.5%

Weighted average for year = 11%

If financial statements were prepared, the total interest income for the year and the total holding gain or loss for the year could be the summation of the four quarterly amounts.

Source: Financial Accounting Standards Board, *An Analysis Related to the Conceptual Framework for Financial Accounting and Reporting: Elements of Financial Statements and Their Measurement, Discussion Memorandum,* Stamford, Conn.: Financial Accounting Standards Board, 1976. Page 217.

EXHIBIT 3-2 **Alternative Current Values of a Bond (Par vs. Discounted Purchase Price)**

January 1, 1976: Purchased a $1,000, 8 percent debenture bond that matures December 31, 1985; interest payments are payable each June 30 and December 31.

Purchased at par

	Asset			*Interest income*	
	Jan. 1, 1976	*Jan. 1, 1981*		*during 1976*	*during 1981*
Historical cost			*Historical cost*		
Face amount	$1,000.00	$1,000.00	Interest payments		
			June 30	$40.00	$40.00
			December 31	40.00	40.00
			Interest income for the year	$80.00	$80.00
*Present value @ 8%**			*Present value*		
Present value of $1,000 maturity payment due December 31, 1985			Interest income		
			January 1–June 30		
(1000 x .456 and 1000 x .676	$ 456.00	$ 676.00	(.04 x 1000)	$40.00	$40.00
Present value of $40 interest payments due at end of each six months			July 1–December 31 (.04 x 1000)	40.00	40.00
(40 x 13.590 and 40 x 8.111)	544.00	324.00			
Total present value @ 8%	$1,000.00	$1,000.00	Interest Income for the year	$80.00	$80.00

EXHIBIT 3–2 *(continued)*

Purchased @ 87 1/2 to yield 10%

	Asset	
	Jan. 1, 1976	*Jan. 1, 1981*
Historical cost and straight-line amortization		
Face amount	$1,000.00	$1,000.00
Less: unamortized discount	125.00	62.50
Amortized cost	$ 875.00	$ 937.50
*Present value @ 10%**		
Present value of $1,000 maturity payment due December 31, 1985 (1000 x .377 and 1000 x .614)	$ 377.00	$ 614.00
Present value of $40 interest payments due at end of each six months (40 x 12.462 and 40 x 7.7222)	498.00	309.00
Total present value @ 10%	$ 875.00	$ 923.00

	Interest income	
	during 1976	*during 1981*
Historical cost and straight-line amortization		
Interest payments		
June 30	$40.00	$40.00
December 31	40.00	40.00
Amortization of discount (straight-line) (1.10 of 125)	12.50	12.50
Interest Income for the year	$92.50	$92.50
Present value		
Interest income January 1–June 30 (.05 x 85 and .05 x 923)	$43.75	$46.15
July 1–December 31 (.05 x 878.75 and .05 x 923	43.94	46.46
Interest Income for the year	$87.69	$92.61

*Because interest payments on bonds are typically made each six months, all present value calculations are based on semiannual interest rates (i.e., one-half the effective or yield rate) and the number of semiannual periods.

Source: Financial Accounting Standards Board, *An Analysis Related to the Conceptual Framework for Financial Accounting and Reporting: Elements of Financial Statements and Their Measurement, Discussion Memorandum*, Stamford, Conn.: Financial Accounting Standards Board, 1976. Page 221.

While the use of the historical rate to measure present value was demonstrated in exhibit 3-2, the use of a current rate at the date of the financial statements is demonstrated in *DM* illustration 3, reproduced here as exhibit 3-3. According to the *DM*, "The use of current rates to measure present value produces holding gains or losses as changes in the applicable current rates occur."[14]

EXHIBIT 3–3 **Alternative Current Values of a Bond (Historical vs. Current Discount Rate)**

January 1, 1976: Purchased a $1,000, 8 percent debenture bond that matures December 31, 1985; interest payments are payable each June 30 and December 31. The bond was purchased at 87 1/2 to yield 10 percent.

January 1, 1981*

Present value at historical rate of 10%:		*Present value at current rate of 12%:*	
Present value of $1,000 maturity payment due December 31, 1985 (1,000 x .614)	$614	Present value of $1,000 maturity payment due December 31, 1985 (1,000 x .558)	$558
Present value of $40 interest payments due at end of each six months (40 x 7.722)	309	Present value of $40 interest payments due at end of each six months (40 x 7.360)	294
Total present value @10%	$923	Total present value @12%	$852

*January 1, 1981: The current rate applicable to the $1,000 debenture bond purchased December 31, 1985 is 12%.

Source: Financial Accounting Standards Board, *An Analysis Related to the Conceptual Framework for Financial Accounting and Reporting: Elements of Financial Statements and Their Measurement, Discussion Memorandum,* Stamford, Conn.: Financial Accounting Standards Board, 1976. Page 224.

The *DM* also included an extensive discussion of the attributes of liabilities. It classified liabilities as Class A, Class B, and Class C: "Class A liabilities are specified amounts of money payable at specified dates, Class B liabilities are estimated amounts of money payable to undesignated members of a class of parties at unknown times within a specified limited time period, and Class C liabilities are products to be delivered or services to be provided."[15] It was noted in the *DM* that the necessary information for measuring the present value of expected cash flows tended to be available for Class A liabilities.

This *DM* contained extensive coverage of present value and its possible application to the valuation of assets and liabilities, although the subsequent statements of concepts contained references to present value which were less extensive. Since the concept statements are intended to be part of an ongoing project, there possibly will be subsequent references to present value.

To date six concept statements have been issued. Since no. 6 superseded no. 3, there are five currently outstanding and applicable concept statements.

Statement of Financial Accounting Concepts, no. 1: Objectives of Financial Reporting by Business Enterprises.

According to its "highlights" section, this *Statement* recognizes that "information often results from approximate, rather than exact, measures" and that "financial reporting should provide information to help investors, creditors, and others assess the amounts, timing, and uncertainty of prospective net cash flows to the related enterprise." It does not address the use of present value or discounting directly except for the following:

> . . . Even the discounted amount of future cash payments required by a long-term debt is, as the name implies, a 'present value' of the liability.[16]

Statement of Financial Accounting Concepts, no. 2: Qualitative Characteristics of Accounting Information.

The purpose of this *Statement* is to examine the characteristics that make accounting information useful. It contends that "the objectives of financial reporting are focused on the use of accounting information in decision making." This *Statement* describes a hierarchy of qualities that make accounting information useful for decision making. It discusses the role of qualities such as relevance, reliability, timeliness, predictive and feedback value, verifiability, representational faithfulness, neutrality, comparability, and consistency. It further contends that the development of accounting information should be guided by cost-benefit analysis of its usefulness and the materiality of its effect. This *Statement* does not address the use of present value or discounting directly except for the following:

> Those who are unfamiliar with the nature of accounting are often surprised at the large number of choices that accountants are required to make. Let choices arise at every turn. Decisions must first be made about the nature and definition of assets and liabilities, revenues and expenses, and the criteria by which they are to be recognized. Then a choice must be made of the attribute of assets to be measured—historical cost, current cost, current exit value, net realizable value, or present value of expected cash flows.

> There are wide variations in the estimates that different people make about the dollar values involved and the rate of discount to be used in reducing them to a present value.[17]

Statement of Financial Accounting Concepts, no. 4: Objectives of Financial Reporting by Nonbusiness Organizations. [18]

This *Statement* establishes the objectives of general purpose external financial reporting by nonbusiness organizations. It contains no direct reference to present value or discounting in this Statement.

Statement of Financial Accounting Concepts, no. 5: Recognition and Measurement in Financial Statements of Business Enterprises.

This *Statement* sets forth criteria and guidance on when and what information should be incorporated into financial statements. It contends that financial statements result from simplifying, condensing, and aggregating masses of data and convey information that would be obscured if great detail were provided. It recognizes that one of the five different attributes of assets and liabilities using current practice is present or discounted value of future cash flows:

> Items currently reported in the financial statements are measured by different attributes (for example, historical cost, current [replacement] cost, current market value, net realizable value, and present value of future cash flows), depending on the nature of the item and the relevance and reliability of the attribute measured. The Board expects use of different attributes to continue.

This *Statement* has the following comment relating to the use of present or discounted value of future cash flows as one of the five attributes of assets and liabilities:

> Long-term receivables are reported at their present value (discounted at the implicit or historical rate) which is the present or discounted value of future cash inflows into which an asset is expected to be converted in due course of business less present values of cash outflows necessary to obtain those inflows. Long-term payables are similarly reported at their present value (discounted at the implicit or historical rate), which is the present or discounted value of future cash outflows expected to be required to satisfy the liability in due course of business.[19]

Statement of Financial Accounting Concepts, no. 6: Elements of Financial Statements.

This Statement replaces *Concepts of Financial Accounting no. 3* and defines ten interrelated elements such as assets, liabilities, and equity that are directly related to measuring the performance and status of an entity. While this did not focus on the use of present value or discounting in financial accounting, it did discuss their use in some circumstances. For example:

> A separate item that reduces or increases the carrying amount of an asset is sometimes found in financial statements. For example, an estimate of uncollectible amounts reduces receivables to the amount expected to be collected, or a premium on a bond receivable increases the receivable to its cost or present value. Those "valuation accounts" are part of the related assets and are neither assets in their own right nor liabilities.
>
> A separate item that reduces or increases the carrying amount of a liability is sometimes found in financial statements. For example, a bond premium or discount increases or decreases the face value of a bond payable to its proceeds or present value. Those "valuation accounts" are part of the related liability and are neither liabilities in their own right nor assets.
>
> *APB* [Accounting Principles Board] *Opinion no. 21*, Interest on Receivables and Payables, changed that practice by requiring debt discount to be (a) deducted directly from the liability (as a "valuation account") and (b) "amortized" by the "interest" method using the effective interest or discount rate implicit in the borrowing transaction. That accounting reports the liability at the present value of the future cash payments for interest and maturity amount, discounted at the effective rate (which is higher than the nominal rate specified in the debt agreement), and reports interest expense at an amount determined by applying the effective rate to the amount of the liability at the beginning of the period." [20]

As this brief review indicates, the *Statements of Financial Accounting Concepts* provide support for the use of discounting in financial accounting. Of the six *Statements*, no. 5 dealt most directly with the use of present value or discounting in financial accounting. It recognized present or discounted value to be one of the five attributes that measure value. The other *Statements* (except no. 4) provide guidance and support for the use of present or discounted value in financial accounting.

L. Todd Johnson and Reed K. Storey authored a Financial Accounting Standards Board (FASB) research report in 1982 as part of the board's accounting recognition project. The project was intended to provide conceptual guidance on when and how to recognize the effects of transactions and other events on an entity's assets, liabilities, and equity. Several areas in that report related to cash flow and present value. For example:

> The value of an asset (or a group of assets) or a liability (or a group of liabilities) at

any time is equal to its present cash consequence (which is the same as its future cash consequences discounted to the present or its past cash consequences accumulated to the present).

A rate of return on an asset reflects both the time value of money and the risk of holding the asset.[21]

In 1987 the AICPA released an *Issues Paper* that covered the use of the present value concept for future non-contractual amounts. Discounting was approached in a general manner, with a focus on loss reserves of property-casualty insurance enterprises and deferred income taxes. Some of the conclusions of this task force were:

1. The present value of future cash flows is the most relevant measurement attribute for the initial recognition of the monetary items with uncertain terms included within the scope of this paper.

2. Discounting should be applied in the initial recognition of monetary items with uncertain terms when the amounts and timing of cash flows are reasonably estimable.

3. If a range of timing of cash flows is known or reasonable estimable, then the most likely data (or period) within that range should be used to compute the present value of future cash flows.

4. The discount rate for assets (liabilities) should be objectively determinable and be the best estimate of the rate at which the monetary assets (liabilities) with uncertain terms could be sold (settled).

5. The discount rate used to determine the present value of future cash flows in the initial recognition of monetary items with uncertain terms (excluding deferred income tax assets and liabilities) should be a before-tax rate.

6. Changes in the estimates of the timing of the cash flows occurring subsequent to the initial recording of monetary items with uncertain terms based on new facts should be recorded as a gain or loss in the income statement unless properly capitalized as part of the cost of an asset.

7. Majority of the task force members believe that changes in the discount rate occurring subsequent to the initial recording of the item should be assessed annually and recognized in the financial statements at that time.

8. The accretion of the present value amount may be reflected as interest expense or interest income, as applicable, or may be combined with the event that gave

rise to the accretion, with appropriate disclosure in the notes to the financial statements.[22]

Conclusions

This chapter has reviewed the discussion of discounting in studies and pronouncements designed to provide guidance for accounting standard setting. Early support for the use of discounting in financial accounting can be said to have started with the 1938 statement of accounting principles. After a twenty-year hiatus, support for the use of discounting again picked up in the late 1950s. Since then, this category of literature designed to provide guidance to the process of setting accounting standards has consistently recognized and recommended the conceptual soundness of the use of discounted present values in financial accounting. In 1973 the FASB initiated the development of a conceptual framework for financial accounting and reporting, an ongoing project that has resulted in an extensive *Discussion Memorandum* and six *Statements of Financial Accounting Standards*. These pronouncements have supported the use of present or discounted values in financial accounting.

Notes

1. Thomas H. Sanders, Henry R. Hatfield, and U. Moore, *Statement of Accounting Principles* (New York: American Institute of Accountants [AICPA], 1938), 70.
2. AAA (American Accounting Association) Committee on Accounting Concepts and Standards, *Accounting and Reporting Standards for Corporate Financial Statements and Preceding Statements and Supplements* (Columbus: AAA, 1957), 4.
3. Maurice Moonitz, *The Basic Postulates of Accounting: Accounting Research Study, [ARS], no. 1* (New York: AICPA, 1961); Robert Sprouse and Maurice Moonitz, *A Tentative Set of Broad Accounting Principles for Business Enterprises: ARS, no. 3* (New York: AICPA, 1962), 24–25.
4. Ibid., 39–40.
5. Paul Grady, *Inventory of Generally Accepted Accounting Principles: ARS, no. 7* (New York: AICPA, 1965), 170, 285.

6. Accounting Principles Board, *Statement no. 4: Basic Concepts and Accounting Principles Underlying Financial Statements of Business Enterprises* (New York: AICPA, 1970), pars. 7, 181.

7. Report of the Study Group on the Objectives of Financial Statements, *Objectives of Financial Statements* (New York: AICPA, 1973).

8. Financial Accounting Standards Board (FASB), *An Analysis Related to the Conceptual Framework for Financial Accounting and Reporting: Elements of Financial Statements and Their Measurement, Discussion Memorandum* (Stamford, Conn.: FASB, 1976).

9. "Scope and Implications of the Conceptual Framework Project," ibid., 16, 17.

10. Ibid., 206.

11. Ibid.

12. Ibid., 215.

13. Ibid., 222.

14. Ibid., 223.

15. Ibid., 239.

16. FASB, *Statement of Financial Accounting Concepts, no. 1: Objectives of Financial Reporting by Business Enterprises* (Stamford, Conn.: FASB, 1978), par. 21.

17. FASB, *Statement of Financial Accounting Concepts, no. 2: Qualitative Characteristics of Accounting Information* (Stamford, Conn.: FASB, 1980), pars. 8, 142.

18. FASB, *Statement of Financial Accounting Concepts, no. 4: Objectives of Financial Reporting by Nonbusiness Organizations* (Stamford, Conn.: FASB, 1980).

19. FASB, *Statement of Financial Accounting Concepts, no. 5: Recognition and Measurement in Financial Statements of Business Enterprises.* (Stamford, Conn.: FASB, 1984), "Highlights," par. 67.

20. FASB, *Statement of Financial Accounting Concepts, no. 6: Elements of Financial Statements,* (Stamford, Conn.: FASB, 1985), par. 34; par. 43; app. B, par. 235.

21. L. Todd Johnson and Reed K. Storey, *Recognition in Financial Statements:*

Underlying Concepts, and Practical Conventions, (Stamford, Conn.: FASB, 1982), 37–38, 58.

22. Task Force on Discounting Applications, Accounting Standards Division, AICPA, *The Use of Discounting in Financial Reporting for Monetary Items with Uncertain Terms Other Than Those Covered by Existing Authoritative Literature, Issues Paper no. 87-2* (New York: AICPA, 1987).

4
Discounting Included in Accounting Standards

Discounting has been included in a number of accounting standards. In this chapter, selected standards issued by the profession and by the Securities and Exchange Commission (SEC) are reviewed with regard to their use of discounting. This review of the use of discounting in accounting standards is intended only to be illustrative.

The first section is a review of accounting standards up to 1972, prior to the issuance of standards by the Financial Accounting Standards Board (FASB) regarding its use of discounting in financial reporting. The second section covers three areas:

1. Discounting in *Statements of Financial Accounting Standards* issued by the FASB.
2. Discounting in the FASB's *Emerging Issues Task Force Issue Releases.*
3. Discounting in *Securities and Exchange Commission Releases.*

Discounting in Early Standards

American Institute of Certified Public Accountants (AICPA), *Accounting Research Bulletin, no. 2: Unamortized Discount and Redemption Premium on Bonds Refunded,* 1939.[1]

This standard, since superseded, recommended the use of discounted present values as the proper approach to record bonds payable. The position was taken that a discount on bonds payable should be treated as part of the cost of borrowed money and that this cost should be distributed systematically over the term of the issue, rather than being immediately written off. It should be noted that this standard did not discuss discounting or the use of present value, but its effect was to introduce discounting to accounting standards.

Accounting Principles Board (APB), *Opinion no. 5: Reporting of Leases in Financial Statements of Lessee,* 1964.[2]

This standard, now superseded, directed that lessees should record lease agreements, which are essentially installment purchases of property, as capital leases. The result is to include property and the related obligation in the balance sheet at the discounted amount of the future lease payments at the time of the lease.

APB, *Opinion no. 8: Accounting for the Cost of Pension Plans,* 1966.[3]

In this standard the use of present value was recognized as influencing the cost assigned to the current period for pension expense under the arrived benefit cost method. This standard has since been superseded by *Statement of Financial Accounting Standards* (SFAS) *no. 87.*

APB, *Opinion no. 10: Omnibus Opinion,* 1966.[4]

In this standard, the question of whether certain long-term tax allocation accounts should be computed on a discounted basis was considered. Pending further consideration of the discounting subject, the board concluded that deferred taxes should not be accounted for on a discounted basis.

APB, *Opinion no. 12: Omnibus Opinion,* 1967.[5]

This *Opinion* found that the use of present value is theoretically sound and is acceptable in determining the minimum accrued amounts for deferred compensation contracts.

APB, *Opinion no. 16: Business Combinations,* 1970.[6]

Present value is used on several occasions in the application of the purchase method.

APB, *Opinion no. 21: Interest on Receivables and Payables,* 1971.[7]

This accounting standard has frequently been referred to in subsequent standards when present value has been addressed. It was a major effort to address present value in accounting standards and remains the only standard to address the general use of present value in financial reporting.

The standard addresses the appropriate accounting when the stated interest rate on a note does not represent the present value of the consideration given or received in an exchange. It is applicable to receivables and payables when there is a contractual obligation to pay or receive money.

There are many exceptions to this standard about which the APB did not take a firm position, including the application of present value to estimates of contractual or other obligations in connection with sales of property, goods, or service. The AICPA's *Issues Paper No. 87-2* addresses the use of present value for noncontractual future amounts (see chapter 3).[8]

The standard addresses: (1) notes exchanged for cash; (2) notes exchanged for property, goods, or service; (3) determination of an appropriate interest rate; (4) amortization of discounts and premiums; and (5) presentation of discounts and premiums in financial statements.

1. *Notes exchanged for cash*

   When a note is received or issued solely for cash it is presumed to have a present value equal to the cash proceeds. If there is some other right or privilege in the exchange, the value of that right or privilege should be recognized.

2. *Notes exchanged for property, goods, or services*

   When a note is exchanged for property, goods, or services, the economic substance should prevail over the form of the transaction. The transaction should be recorded at face value of the property, goods, or services or the market value of the note, whichever is more clearly determinable. In the absence of an established face value of the property, goods, or services or a market value of the note, the transaction should be recorded at the present value of the note. The present value should be determined by discounting the note using the imputed rate of interest.

3. *Determination of an appropriate interest rate*

   The appropriate interest rate should be determined by considering factors such as the credit standing of the issuer, collateral, and payment terms. The objective is to determine the rate that an independent borrower and independent lender would have agreed to.

4. *Amortization of discounts and premiums*

   Amortization should result in a constant rate over the life of the note when applied to the amount outstanding at the beginning of any given period.

5. *Presentation of discounts and premiums in statements*

   The discount or premium should be on the balance sheet as a direct deduction from or addition to the face amount of the note. Amortization of the discount or premium is reported as interest in the income statement. It should be noted that the use of present value in this standard relates to the date of the original transaction. Subsequent changes in the imputed rate are ignored.

Discounting in Recent Accounting Standards

The FASB's *Statement of Financial Accounting Standards*

Statement of Financial Accounting Standards, (SFAS) no. 13: Accounting for Leases, 1976.[9]

This standard prescribes procedures for the financial accounting and reporting of leases by lessees and lessors, and provides for the use of present value by both. The lessee records a capital lease at present value, using the minimum lease payments during the lease term and excluding that portion of the lease payments representing executory costs. The lessor records the present value of the minimum lease payments, net of executory costs, as the sales price of sales-type leases. The *Statement* does not use interest methods in valuing operating leases or in leveraged lease accounting.

SFAS, no. 15: Accounting by Debtors and Creditors for Troubled Debt Restructurings, 1977.

This standard does not provide for the use of present value at the time of restructuring of troubled debt by either the debtor or the creditor. However, it does call for interest to be computed in years subsequent to the restructuring by using the "interest method" prescribed by the APB's *Opinion no. 21.*[10]

SFAS, no. 33: Financial Reporting and Changing Prices, 1979.

SFAS no. 33, since superseded, included several references to the use of present value. For example:

> Net present value of expected future cash flows. Assets are measured at the present value of expected future cash inflows into which the asset is expected to be converted in due course of business less the present value of expected future cash outflows necessary to obtain those inflows. This measurement of an asset is often described as value in use. (Paragraph 99, Appendix)

> Current cost represents a conservative measure of the net present value of future cash flows because net present value represents the maximum price at which purchase of an asset would be worthwhile.

Some Board members concluded that the measurement of assets at current cost or lower recoverable amount could provide a useful basis for assessing future cash flows to the enterprise because those measurements can be regarded as surrogates for the net present value of cash flows expected to be earned from the use of assets. Current costs may presumably be expected to have some relationship to net present values (and hence future cash flows) because estimated net present value will represent the maximum sum that an enterprise would be willing to pay for an asset. The exact nature of the relationship will depend on conditions in the markets in which the assets are bought and sold. Measurements of assets at their recoverable amounts represent direct estimates of the net present values of future cash flows (in the case of values in use) or approximations to net present values (in the case of net realizable values).[11]

SFAS, no. 35: Accounting and Reporting by Defined Benefit Pension Plans, 1980.

This standard calls for the primary information regarding participants' accumulated plan benefits to be reported at their actuarial present value. Accumulated plan benefits are adjusted to reflect both the probability of payments and the time value of money. The standard also contains other references to present value. For example:

> Plan investments, whether equity or debt securities, real estate, or other (excluding contracts with insurance companies) shall be presented at their fair value at the reporting date. The fair value of an investment is the amount that the plan could reasonably expect to receive for it in a current sale between a willing buyer and a willing seller, that is, other than a forced liquidation sale. Fair value shall be measured by the market price if there is an active market for the investment. If there is not an active market for the investment but there is such a market for similar investments, selling prices in that market may be helpful in estimating fair value. If a market price is not available, a forecast of expected cash flows may aid in estimating fair value, provided the expected cash flows are discounted at a rate commensurate with the risk involved.[12]

SFAS, no. 38: Accounting for Pre-acquisition Contingencies of Purchased Enterprises, 1980.

The board concluded that it should not specify a present value computation for pre-acquisition contingencies of purchased enterprises because the timing of payment or receipt of a contingent item seldom would be sufficiently determinable to permit the use of a present value technique on a reasonable basis. However, this statement does not prohibit the use of a present value if appropriate.[13]

SFAS, no. 43: Accounting for Compensated Absences, 1980.

This *Statement* requires an employer to accrue a liability for employees' rights to receive compensation for future absences. The board did not take a firm position on the use of present value:

> Some respondents requested guidance on how an employer should estimate its liability for compensated absences. The respondents asked (a) whether the liability should be based on current or on future rate of pay, (b) whether it should be discounted, and (c) when the effect of scheduled increases should be accrued. The Board noted that it expects to be studying similar issues in its project on accounting by employers for pensions as well as in a possible project on discounting and, accordingly, concluded to defer a decision on such issues at this time.[14]

SFAS, no. 47: Disclosure of Long Term-Obligations, 1981.

This *Statement* requires that an enterprise disclose its commitments under unconditional purchase obligations that are associated with suppliers' financing arrangements. This *Statement* encourages the use of present value:

> Disclosure of the amount of imputed interest necessary to reduce the unconditional purchase obligation(s) to present value is encouraged but not required. The discount rate shall be the effective initial interest rate of the borrowings that financed the facility (or facilities) that will provide the contracted goods or services, if known by the purchaser. If not, the discount rate shall be the purchaser's incremental borrowing rate at the date the obligation is entered into.[15]

SFAS, no. 60: Accounting and Reporting by Insurance Enterprises, 1982.

This *Statement* extracts the specialized principles and practices from the AICPA's insurance industry–related *Guides* and *Statements of Position.* It recognizes the use of present value in some situations. For example:

> Premiums from long-duration contracts shall be recognized as revenue when due from policyholders. . . . The present value of estimated future policy benefits to be paid to or on behalf of policyholders less the present value of estimated future net premiums to be collected from policyholders (liability for future policy benefits) shall be accrued when premium revenue is recognized. Those estimates shall be based on assumptions, such as estimates of expected investment yields, mortality, morbidity, terminations, and expenses, applicable at the time the insurance contracts are made.[16]

This *Statement* also covers situations in which discounting is not used, such as in accounting for claim liabilities related to contracts of short duration even though the claims may not be asserted and paid for a number of years.

SFAS, no. 65: Accounting for Certain Mortgage Banking Activities, 1982.

This *Statement* extracts the specialized accounting and reporting principles from the AICPA's *Statements of Position 74-12* and *76-2*[17] and establishes the accounting and reporting standards for certain mortgage banking activities. It provides guidelines for the use of present value. For example:

> The amount capitalized as the right to service mortgage loans shall not exceed the amount by which the present value of estimated future servicing revenue exceeds the present value of expected future servicing costs . . . The rate to be used to determine the present value shall be an appropriate long-term interest rate.[18]

SFAS, no. 66: Accounting for Sales of Real Estate, 1982.

This *Statement* establishes accounting standards for recognizing profit or loss on sales of real estate. In such disclosures, it provides for the use of present value. For example:

> The present value of the specified rental payments is the present value of the lease payments specified in the lease over the term of the primary indebtedness, if any, on the improvements, or over the customary amortization term of primary debt instruments on the type of improvements involved. The present value is computed at an interest rate appropriate for (a) primary debt if the lease is not subordinated or (b) secondary debt if the lease is subordinated to loans with prior liens.
>
> The net receivable is discounted to the present value of the payments required. The present value is determined using an appropriate interest rate, not less than the rate stated in the sales contract. The objective is to value the net receivable at the amount at which it could be sold without recourse to the seller at the date of the sales contract.
>
> In determining the amount of unrecoverable costs, estimates of amounts to be recovered from future sale of the improvements, utilities, and amenities are discounted to present value as of the date the net unrecoverable costs are recognized.[19]

SFAS, no. 69: Disclosures about Oil and Gas Producing Activities, 1982.

This *Statement* establishes a comprehensive set of disclosures for oil and gas producing activities. In such disclosures, it requires the use of present value in measuring proven oil and gas reserves. For example:

> A standardized measure of discounted future net cash flows relating to an enterprise's interest in (a) proved oil and gas reserves (paragraph 10) and (b) oil and gas subject to purchase under long-term supply, purchase, or similar agreements and contracts in which the enterprise participates in the operation of the properties

on which the oil or gas is located or otherwise serves as the producer of those reserves (paragraph 13) shall be disclosed as of the end of the year.[20]

SFAS, no. 71: Accounting for the Effects of Certain Types of Regulation, 1982.[21]

This *Standard* provides guidance in preparing general purpose financial statements for most public utilities. While the following paragraph has been superseded by *Statement No. 90,*[22] according to *Statement No. 71:*

> The regulator's action provides reasonable assurance of the existence of an asset (paragraph 9). Accordingly, the regulated enterprise would capitalize the incurred cost and amortize it over the period during which it will be allowed for ratemaking purposes. That cost would not be recorded at discounted present value. If the amounts are material, the disclosures specified in paragraph 20 of this Statement would be furnished.[23]

SFAS, no. 87: Employers' Accounting for Pensions, 1985.[24]

The board believed that the most relevant and reliable information relating to pension obligations would be based on the fair value of the pension plan assets and a present value of the obligation. While it concluded that recognition in financial statements of these amounts in their entirety would be too great a change in practice, the board did agree to increased reporting of pension plans, including a partial recognition of the estimated liability. The standard uses present value in determining pension expense, pension obligations, and footnote disclosure.

For example, part of the pension expense under a defined pension plan is the increase in the projected benefit obligation due to the passage of time. Part of the pension liability recognized comes from the comparison of accumulated benefit obligation with the fair value of the plans assets. The pension disclosure includes the projected benefit obligation. Both the projected benefit obligation and the accumulated benefit obligation are determined using a present value computation.

SFAS, no. 88: Employers' Accounting for Settlements and Curtailments of Defined Benefit Pension Plans and for Termination Benefits, 1985.[25]

This *Statement* supersedes *Statement no. 74* and is closely related to *Statement no. 87.* It should be considered in that context. *Statement 88* was developed in response to an increase in the number of companies engaging in settlements and curtailments of pension plans or companies terminating pension plans whose assets were in excess of the plan's accumulated benefits. The present value of expected future payments along with any changes in estimates of these present values are to be included in the costs of settlements, curtailments, or termination benefits, recognized as liabilities.

SFAS no. 89: Financial Reporting and Changing Prices, 1985.[26]

Appendix A of this standard includes guidance for the measurement and presentation of supplementary information on the effect of changing prices. This guidance indicated that the unguaranteed residual value of a lesser's sales type or leveraged lease should be considered at present value in the net investment in the lease.

SFAS no. 90: Regulated Enterprises, Accounting for Abandonment and Disallowance of Plant Costs, 1985.[27]

This *Statement* addresses abandonments of plants and disallowances of costs of recently completed plants in the electric utility industry. Revenue that is expected to result from the inclusion of the cost of an abandoned plant in the rate-making process is required to be reported at its present value when the abandonment becomes probable. At that time, if the abandoned plant's cost exceeds the present value of the future revenue, a loss is recognized.

SFAS no. 91: Accounting for Nonrefundable Fees and Costs Associated with Originating or Acquiring Loans and Initial Direct Costs of Leases, 1986.[28]

This *Statement* establishes the accounting for nonrefundable fees and costs associated with lending, committing to lend, or purchasing a loan or group of loans. It provides for an initial investment in a purchased loan or group of loans to include the amount paid to the seller plus any fees paid or less any fees received.

Some of the items specified in this statement are:

1. Loan origination fees shall be recognized over the life of the related loan as an adjustment of yield.
2. Certain direct loan origination costs shall be recognized over the life of the related loan as a reduction of the loan's yield.
3. Many commitment fees shall be recognized as an adjustment of yield over the related loan's life.
4. Loan fees, certain direct loan origination costs, and purchase premiums and discounts on loans shall be recognized as an adjustment of yield.

SFAS no. 96: Accounting for Income Taxes, 1987.[29]

This *Statement* addresses the financial accounting and reporting standards for the effects of income taxes. The Board considered whether a deferred tax liability or asset should be determined on a present value basis. As in *Opinion No. 10*, issued in 1966, because the conceptual and implementation issues associated with discounting in this area are complex, the board once again decided not to resolve those issues at the time. It thereby continued the prohibition against the use of discounting in accounting for deferred taxes.

SFAS no. 97: Accounting and Reporting by Insurance Enterprises for Certain Long-Duration Contracts and for Realized Gains and Losses from the Sale of Investments, 1987.[30]

The *Statement* defines the accounting methods to be used for several classifications of long-duration life insurance and annuity products. The *Statement* calls for acquisition costs for universal life-type policies to be deferred and amortized in relation to the present value of estimated future gross profits.

FASB Technical Bulletins

A number of these *Bulletins* that clarify certain aspects of FASB standards have also addressed the use of interest methods in financial accounting. For example, both the *Technical Bulletin, no. 85-3: Accounting for Operating Leases with Scheduled Rent Increases or the Technical Bulletin, no. 85-4, Accounting for Purchases of Life Insurance* prohibit the use of present value.[31] However, a complete discussion of these various *Bulletins* is beyond the scope of this study.

The FASB's Emerging Issues Task Force's Releases

The FASB established the Emerging Issues Task Force in July 1984, to assist the board in the early identification of emerging issues. The task force of fifteen members include senior technical partners of major national CPA firms and representatives of major associations of preparers of financial statements.

An agreement of the task force is recognized as a consensus if no more than two members disagree with a position. The SEC's chief accountant has taken the position that the SEC would challenge any accounting policy that differs from a consensus.

Emerging Issue Task Force, *Issue no. 84-21: Sale of Loan with a Partial Participation Retained.* Dates discussed: September 25, 1984; December 13, 1984.[32]

The issue was whether the present value of the estimated future interest income stream should be recognized immediately in calculating a gain or loss on the sale of a loan or recognized over the life of the loan. The task force was unable to reach a consensus on this issue.

Issue no. 84-28: Impairment of Long Lived Assets. Dates discussed: October 18, 1984; December 19, 1985; February 6, 1986.[33]

The issue was the Generally Accepted Accounting Principles for determining whether a write-down should be recorded in assessing the impairment of productive assets. The task force was unable to reach a consensus. The SEC observer noted that the SEC would accept, but not require, recognition of impairment based on the discounting of future cash flows.

Issue no. 85-15: Recognizing Benefits of Purchased Net Operating Loss Carryforwards. Dates discussed: May 9, 1985; June 27, 1985.[34]

The issue relates to a historically profitable company acquiring another entity that has an unrecognized net operating loss carryforward that can be used against the future income tax liability of the acquirer. The acquisition is recorded as a purchase. The task force was unable to reach a consensus on whether the benefit should be recognized at its gross amount or at a discounted amount.

Issue No. 85-24: Distribution Fees by Distributors of Mutual Funds That Do Not Have a Front-End Sales Charge. Dates discussed: June 27, 1985; February 6, 1986.[35]

Distributors of mutual funds that do not have a front-end sales charge sometimes receive fees over a specified future period. The task force considered whether the fees that are expected to be received in future periods should be accrued at present value and recognized at the time of distribution, along with all costs of performance. This method was rejected by the task force.

Issue no. 86-17: Deferred Profit on Sale-Leaseback Transaction with Lessee Guarantee of Residual Value. Dates discussed: June 12, 1986; September 4, 1986.[36]

The issue involved sale-leaseback transactions in which the seller-lessee guarantees to the lessor that the residual value will be a stipulated amount. The sales-leaseback does not meet the criteria for classification as a capital lease and the seller-lessee retains more than a minor part, but less than substantially all, of the use of the property. A consensus was reached that profit equal to the present value of the periodic rents, plus the gross amount of the guarantee, should be deferred at the date of sale. The deferred gross amount of the guarantee should remain deferred until the guarantee is resolved. The deferred profit equal to the present value of the periodic rents should be amortized in relation to subsequent gross rental expense. This release was superceded by *SFAS no. 98.*

Issue no. 86-18: Debtor's Accounting for a Modification of Debt Terms.

Dates discussed: June 12, 1986; September 4, 1986; October 16, 1986; January 15, 1987.[37]

Debtors may consider transactions that would use the leverage of an existing call provision to reduce the higher interest rate on an older debt issue. This would include having the creditor pay a fee in return for an agreement not to exercise the call provision. The task force considered the present value of the originally scheduled cash flows compared with the present value of the cash flows under the modified terms but, could not reach an agreement regarding accounting for fees paid for a waiver of a call option.

Issue no. 86-24: Third-Party Establishment of Collateralized Mortgage Obligations. Dates discussed: September 4, 1986; October 16, 1986; February 26, 1987.[38]

The issue involves the sale of mortgage loans by a financial institution to an unrelated third party who then uses the mortgages as collateral to issue collateralized mortgage obligations. The financial institution acquires the right to receive a defined portion of the total payments received from the mortgages in excess of the amount required to service the collateralized mortgage obligations.

The task force reached a consensus that the present value of the residual interest should be recognized as part of the gain or loss recognized in the period in which the transaction occurs.

Issue no. 86-38: Implications of Mortgage Prepayments on Amortization of Servicing Rights. Dates discussed: December 4, 1986; May 21, 1987; August 20, 1987.[39]

1. Unanticipated prepayments and purchased mortgage servicing rights.

    If the enterprise experiences unanticipated mortgage prepayments, the enterprise must adjust its amortization. One of the issues is whether discounting should be considered. The task force reached a consensus that the evaluation could be based on either a discounted or undiscounted future net servicing income, depending on the method used to evaluate other similar intangible assets.

2. Unanticipated prepayments and receivables for excess service fees.

    The issue is how the enterprise should record the adjustment and whether discounting should be considered. The task force reached a consensus that the write-down should be to the present value of the estimated remaining future excess service fee. An adjustment would not be made as a result of favorable prepayment experience.

Issue no. 87-2: Net Present Value Method of Valuing Speculative Foreign Exchange Contracts. Dates discussed: February 26, 1987; April 7, 1987.[40]

The issue is whether the discounting approach should be used in calculating the gain or loss on unsettled speculative foreign currency forward exchange contracts. The task force reached a consensus that discounting is allowed but not required.

Issue no. 87-11: Allocation of Purchase Price to Assets to Be Sold. Dates discussed: May 21, 1987; July 9, 1987; August 20, 1987; October 1, 1987.[41]

An enterprise may acquire another firm in an acquisition accounted for as a purchase. It may intend to sell one or more operating units of the acquired firm to pay for the purchase. One of the issues is whether the estimated proceeds from the projected sales should be discounted in determining the purchase price allocation. If the projected sales are discounted, should there be subsequent accretion from the acquisition date to the date of sale? The task force did not reach a consensus, but the majority of its members indicated that the estimated proceeds from sales of operating units could be discounted and subsequently accrued.

Issue no. 87-19: Substituted Debtors in a Troubled Debt Restructuring. Date discussed: July 9, 1987.[42]

The issue is whether the creditor should recognize a loss when the debtor sells real estate on a contract where the present value is less than the creditor's net investment in the related loan. The task force reached a consensus that the creditor should recognize a loss and record an asset for the fair value of the payments to be received.

Securities and Exchange Commission Releases

In the United States, the SEC has the legal authority to issue accounting rules for publicly owned companies. In general, the SEC has delegated to the accounting profession the leading role in issuing accounting standards. However, accounting rules issued by the SEC have established the accounting standards for publicly traded companies in those cases in which the SEC believes that the accounting standards established by the private sector do not sufficiently address an SEC concern. A review of the accounting rules issued by the SEC revealed that, in at least two areas, the SEC included present value as part of the rule making. These areas relate to the disclosure of leases and reporting practices for oil and gas producing activities.

In 1973, the SEC issued *Accounting Series, Release no. 147,* which required improved disclosure of leases.[43] The Accounting Principles Board had previously issued *Opinion no. 31* in June 1973, covering the same area.[44] However, the SEC concluded that the requirements in *Opinion 31* provided insufficient disclosure for the investor's needs. Specifically, the SEC, in *Release no. 147* issued on October 5, 1973, considered "that disclosure of the present value of financing leases and of the impact on net income of capitalizing such leases" was necessary.[45]

The second area where the SEC required the use of present values was in the accounting and reporting of oil and gas producing activities. The SEC concluded that data supplemental to financial statements are necessary in this area and issued *Release no. 253* on August 31, 1978.[46] This *Release* required that such additional data that should be disclosed should include the "present value of net revenue from estimated future production of proven oil and gas reserves using a ten percent discount rate."[47] The SEC elaborated on this position in a number of subsequent releases.

Conclusions

The first use of discounting in accounting standards issued by the accounting profession came in 1939 in the presentation of unamortized discount when a bond is issued. It should be noted that the effect of this standard was to introduce the discounting methodology to accounting standards even though that standard did not discuss discounting. The first standard that deliberately used discounting was the standard on reporting of leases issued in 1964.[48]

A review of the recent influence of discounting on accounting standards issued by the accounting profession indicates that consideration of discounting has been frequent and seems to have followed its discussion in the academic literature. Several recent *Statements of Financial Accounting Standards* have used or considered using discounting.

The FASB's Emerging Issues Task Force has frequently considered the appropriateness of discounting to specific financial reporting issues. In many of these cases they arrived at a consensus that included discounting.

The SEC also has included the use of present values as part of its accounting releases in at least two cases. These relate to disclosures regarding leases and to the reporting for oil and gas producing activities.[49]

Discussions of the appropriateness of discounting in specific accounting standards have become frequent. Unfortunately, there is limited overall guidance on this issue in accounting standards and the standard setting process is left only with the general guideline that money in the future is worth less today. Because of this limited guidance, some have contended that the use of discounting in accounting standards has been ad hoc in nature and that it has led to a number of inconsistencies in the treatment of different events in financial reporting. In the next chapter, we briefly review some of these problems.

Notes

1. American Institute of Certified Public Accountants (AICPA), *Accounting Research Bulletin, no. 2: Unamortized Discount and Redemption Premium on Bonds Refunded* (New York, AICPA, 1939).
2. Accounting Principles Board, (APB), *Opinion no. 5: Reporting of Leases in Financial Statements of Lessee* (New York: AICPA, 1964).
3. ———. *Opinion no. 8: Accounting for the Cost of Pension Plans* (New York: AICPA, 1966).
4. ———. *Opinion no. 10: Omnibus Opinion* (New York: AICPA, 1966).
5. ———. *Opinion no. 12: Omnibus Opinion* (New York AICPA, 1967).
6. ———. *Opinion no.16: Business Combinations* (New York: AICPA, 1970).
7. ———. *Opinion no. 21: Interest on Receivables and Payables* (New York: AICPA, 1970).
8. Task Force on Discounting Applications, Accounting Standards Division, AICPA, *Issue Paper 87-2: The Use of Discounting in Financial Reporting for Monetary Items with Uncertain Terms Other Than Those Covered by Existing Authoritative Literature* (New York: AICPA, 1987).
9. Financial Accounting Standards Board [FASB], *Statement of Financial Standards, no 13: Accounting for Leases* (Stamford: Conn.: FASB, 1976).
10. ———. *Statement of Financial Accounting Standards [SFAS], no. 15: Accounting by Debtors and Creditors for Troubled Debt Restructuring* (Stamford, Conn.: FASB, 1977).
11. ———. *SFAS, no. 33: Financial Reporting for Changing Prices* (Stamford, Conn.: FASB, 1979), app., pars. 99, 120, 133.
12. ———. *SFAS, no. 35: Accounting and Reporting by Defined Benefit Plans* (Stamford, Conn.: FASB, 1980), par. 11.

13. ———. *SFAS, no. 38: Accounting for Pre-Acquisition Contingencies of Purchased Enterprises* (Stamford, Conn.: FASB, 1980), app. B, par. 33.

14. ———. *SFAS, no. 43: Accounting for Compensated Absences* (Stamford, Conn.: FASB, 1980), app. A, par. 20.

15. ———. *SFAS, no. 47: Disclosure of Long-Term Obligations* (Stamford, Conn.: FASB, 1981), par. 8.

16. ———. *SFAS, no. 60: Accounting and Reporting by Insurance Companies* (Stamford, Conn.: FASB, 1982), par. 10.

17. AICPA, *Statement of Position 74-12* (New York: AICPA, 1974); *Statement of Position 76-2* (New York: AICPA, 1976).

18. Financial Accountaing Standards Board, *SFAS, no 65: Accounting for Certain Mortgage Banking Activities* (Stamford, Conn.: FASB, 1982), par. 18.

19. ———. *SFAS, no 66: Accounting for Sales of Real Estate* (Stamford, Conn.: FASB, 1982), fn. 15, app. B, pars, 70, 75.

20. ———. *SFAS, no 69: Accounting for Oil and Gas Exploration Activities* (Stamford, Conn.: FASB, 1982), par. 30.

21. ———. *SFAS, no 71: Accounting for the Effects of Certain Types of Regulation* (Stamford, Conn.: FASB, 1982).

22. ———. *SFAS, no. 90: Regulated Enterprises—Accounting for Abandonment and Disallowance of Plant Costs* (Stamford, Conn.: FASB, 1985).

23. ———. *SFAS, no. 71*, app. B, par. 34.

24. ———. *SFAS, no. 87*, 1985.

25. ———. *SFAS, no. 88: Employers' Accounting for Settlements and Curtailments of Defined Benefit Pension Plans and for Termination Benefits* (Stamford, Conn.: FASB, 1985).

26. ———, *SFAS, no. 89: Financial Reporting and Changing Prices* (Stamford, Conn.: FASB, 1985), app. A.

27. ———. *SFAS, no. 90: Regulated Enterprises—Accounting for Abandonment and Disallowance of Plant Costs* (Stamford, Conn.: FASB, 1985).

28. ———. *SFAS, no. 91: Accounting for Nonrefundable Fees and Costs Associated with Originating or Acquiring Loans and Initial Direct Costs of Leases* (Stamford, Conn.: FASB, 1986).

29. ———. *SFAS, no. 96: Accounting for Income Taxes* (Stamford, Conn.: FASB, 1987.

30. ———. *SFAS, no. 97: Accounting and Reporting by Insurance Enterprises for Certain Long-Duration Contracts and for Realized Gains and Losses from the Sale of Investments* (Stamford, Conn.: FASB, 1987).

31. ———. *Technical Bulletin, no. 85-3: Accounting for Operating Leases with Scheduled Rent Increases* (Stamford, Conn.: FASB, 1985); *Technical Bulletin, no. 85-4: Accounting for Purchases of Life Insurance* (Stamford, Conn.: FASB, 1985).

32. ———. Emerging Issue Task Force, *Issue no. 84-21: Sale or Loan with a Partial Participation Retained* (Stamford, Conn.: FASB, 1984).

33. ———. Emerging Issue Task Force, *Issue no. 84-28: Impairment of Long Lived Assets* (Stamford, Conn.: FASB, 1984).

34. ———. Emerging Issue Task Force, *Issue no. 85-15: Recognizing Benefits of Purchased Net Operating Loss Carryforwards* (Stamford, Conn.: FASB, 1985).

35. ———. Emerging Issue Task Force, *Issue no. 85-24: Distribution Fees by Distributors of Mutual Funds That Do Not Have a Front-End Sales Charge* (Stamford, Conn.: FASB, 1985).

36. ———. Emerging Issue Task Force, *Issue no. 86-17: Deferred Profit on Sale-Leaseback Transaction with Lessee Guarantee of Residual Value* (Stamford, Conn.: FASB, 1986).

37. ———. Emerging Issue Task Force, *Issue no. 86-18: Debtor's Accounting for Modification of Debt Terms* (Stamford, Conn.: FASB, 1986).

38. ———. Emerging Issue Task Force, *Issue no. 86-24: Third-Party Establishment of Collateralized Mortgage Obligations* (Stamford, Conn.: FASB, 1986).

39. ———. Emerging Issue Task Force, *Issue no. 86-38; Implications of Mortgage Prepayments on Amortization of Servicing Rights* (Stamford, Conn.: FASB, 1986).

40. ———. Emerging Issue Task Force, *Issue no. 87-2: Net Present Value Method of Valuing Speculative Foreign Exchange Contracts* (Stamford, Conn.: FASB, 1987).

41. ———. Emerging Issue Task Force, *Issue no. 87-11: Allocation of Purchase Price to Assets to Be Sold* (Stamford, Conn.: FASB, 1987).

42. ———. Emerging Issue Task Force, *Issue no. 87-19: Substituted Debtors in a Troubled Debt Restructuring* (Stamford, Conn.: FASB, 1987).

43. Securities and Exchange Commission (SEC), *Accounting Series, Release no. 147: Requirements for Improved Disclosure of Leases* (Washington, D.C.: Government Printing Office, 1973).

44. APB, *Opinion no. 31: Disclosure of Lease Commitments by Lessees* (New York: AICPA, 1973).

45. SEC *Release no. 147,* as reported in the Commerce Clearing House, *Federal Securities Law Reports*, page 62, 335.

46. ———. *Accounting Series, Release, no. 253, Financial Accounting and Reporting Practices for Oil and Gas Producing Activities* (Washington, D.C.: Government Printing Office, 1978).

47. Ibid., as reported in the Commerce Clearing House, *Federal Securities Law Reports,* page 62, 746.

48. APB, *Opinion no. 5: Reporting of Leases in Financial Statements,* (AICPA: New York 1964).

49. SEC, *Accounting Series Release, nos. 43, 147.*

5
Examples of Problems in Applying Discounting

The first section of this chapter is a review of some of the problems in applying discounts that we discussed in books and articles; the second section, of problems encountered in accounting standards and pronouncements. Examples of the problems are given to convey the essence of the issues involved.

Examples from Accounting Literature

In this section, we cover the use of discounting in five major areas; deferred taxes, pensions, asset utilization, depreciation, and oil and gas accounting.

Deferred Taxes

In a 1957 paper, Thomas Hill contended that the liability for future tax payments could not be meaningfully stated at the absolute dollar amount of the expected future outlay. Hill recommended that the present value of such amounts be determined using rates established in the financial markets.[1]

Hugo Nurnberg authored a paper in 1972, examining the arguments for and against accounting for deferred tax liabilities on a discounted basis. He also discussed the rate of discount to be used. The argument against the use of discounting was that, other things being equal, the firm pays the same taxes with or without deferring them and that a deferred tax liability represents an interest-free loan. The argument for the use of discounting was that not to recognize interest is a departure from the usual concept of interest expense applicable to other liabilities and that deferred tax liabilities should be reported on a discounted basis.[2]

Edward E. Williams and M. Chapman Findlay III published a follow-up to

Nurnberg's article. They agreed with his position that deferred taxes represent an interest-free loan from the government which should increase net worth and be reported in income. However, they took exception to Nurnberg in several respects. They took the position that the discount rate should be the cost of equity, K_e, times 1 minus the tax rate, $(1–t)$—that is, $K_e(1–t)$—and that the determination of the amount of incremental income and its temporal distribution would depend on whether deferred taxes are treated as debt or as equity.[3]

In 1973, Stephen L. Meyers analyzed the underlying conflict between present value depreciation and interperiod tax allocation. One of his recommendations was that depreciation of present value be based on pre-tax benefits anticipated from depreciable assets. Such an approach, he felt, would make the two concepts consistent with each other and with Generally Accepted Accounting Principles.[4]

James E. Wheeler and Willard H. Galliart prepared a research study for the Financial Executives Research Foundation in 1974, titled *An Appraisal of Interperiod Income Tax Allocation.* They reviewed the possibility of presenting interperiod income tax allocation at the discounted amount, recognizing that a body of literature supports the use of discounting in interperiod income tax allocation. It is supported as a means of determining the "burden" of tax deferral and as a means of allocating the tax cost between years. It was also noted that some of the leading critics of comprehensive tax allocation have supported discounting of deferred taxes.

Wheeler and Galliart argued for the need for a thorough consideration of the strengths and weaknesses of reporting deferred taxes on a discounted basis. Such a review should take into account three factors:

1. What is to be discounted?
2. What is the length of the discount period?
3. What discount rate is appropriate?

The authors discussed the problem of estimating these factors, rejected the recommendation for using the internal earnings rate made in *Accounting Research Study* no. 9, questioned the ability of the readers of financial statements to understand the significance of discounted deferred taxes, and thought that the resulting financial statements would be less valuable. They concluded against the use of discounting.[5]

Harry I. Wolk and Michael G. Tearney reviewed the issues related to the deferral of tax liabilities in 1980. They concluded that deferred taxes were a liability and that the appropriate discount rate would appear to be the rate applicable to an unsecured obligation of similar maturity with a premium added for uncertainty.[6]

In 1981, Kenneth Lemke and Paul R. Graul proposed a method of measuring deferred tax liabilities on a discounted present value basis. They concluded that the rates of return expected on the firm's future investments should be used to compute their present value.[7]

In 1985, James D. Stepp discussed the issue of discounting deferred taxes. He concluded against discounting for conceptual reasons and because of problems of application. His conceptual objections were related to the fact that the amount and timing of the tax payable would depend on the tax rates enacted for future time periods and the taxpayer's tax position, and the fact that no interest is due on deferred taxes. His list of problems in application included the increased complexity and computational effort required by discounting and the difficulties of choosing the correct rate and time period for discounting.[8]

M. C. Findlay and E. E. Williams wrote a paper that carried on the debate about whether deferred tax liabilities should be discounted at pre-tax rates or after-tax rates. They took the position that deferred tax liabilities should be discounted at after-tax rates and claimed that the discount rate used should be an after-tax rate.[9]

A 1987 paper by Sudro Brown and Jeffrey Lippitt included a summary of past articles addressing discounting of deferred taxes. The purpose of this paper was to continue the examination of the nature of deferred taxes. Their analysis centered on the procedures for applying the discount rate and on a numerical example. In an earlier paper, F. Rayburn had reviewed the authoritative literature on interperiod tax allocation from 1940 to 1985.[10]

Pension Liabilities

In 1986, Richard A. Ippolito described the theory behind pension liabilities, concluding that reported pension liabilities fell short of the true liabilities incurred by firms. A portion of this paper was devoted to a discussion of the proper discount rate to use when estimating pension liabilities. An approach considered was to assume that the stock market correctly calculates pension liabilities by using economic discount rates. This approach indicated that the best estimate of the discount rate used by the stock market to evaluate true pension liabilities is 2 percent, since growth in pension liabilities due to inflation is expected to offset all but 2 percent of the average long-run growth of pension assets.[11]

In 1987, John Maher discussed the disclosure of defined benefit pension plans. Measurement of the future pension obligation is determined, in large part, by a company-chosen discount rate. The empirical analysis presented in this paper provided evidence of whether a pension obligation measure is impounded in bond ratings. The results supported the idea that bond rating analysts are not fooled by the use of high interest rates by some companies to minimize the reported pension obligation.[12]

In two 1987 articles, contradictory positions were taken on the practicality of *Statement of Financial Accounting Standard, SFAS no. 87*. Since pension cost calculations are very sensitive to changes in the discount rate, one of the arguments presented against this standard was the resulting volatility of the income statement due to the requirement to use the current interest rate for discounting. It was argued that the recommended procedures for choosing the discount rate were not relevant. The paper favoring the standard included an argument that the criticism regarding volatility is overemphasized because the standard contains several mechanisms for limiting volatility.[13]

Another author to address *SFAS no. 87* was Nancy Connors, who pointed out that the *Standard* requires the present value of an employee's pension benefits be based on length of service, then that the distributed cost be based on the actual value of the pension in any given year of the employee's service. The *Standard* also requires companies to re-estimate future earnings on pension assets each year because of changes in interest rates. Another 1987 article that addressed *SFAS no. 87* (but not the use of present values) was written by Joseph C. Rue and David E. Tosh. They explored some of the theoretical and practical problems associated with the standard, and concluded that the standard has some reporting requirements which are difficult to defend either on strict theoretical or practical grounds.[14]

Asset Valuation

William J. Morris and Bernard A. Coda discussed long-term investments in marketable equity securities of such entities as insurance companies and pension funds, in 1973. They concluded that the use of current market value for long-term investments is not warranted and that the best available net realizable value is the accounting method with the minimum deviation from the ideal of using the present value of future cash proceeds.[15]

In 1974, Arthur R. Wyatt demonstrated the case for capitalization of leases, observing that the present value of financial leases should be disclosed along with the effect of lease capitalization on reported net income. In 1979, Gadis J. Dillon examined the implications of estimating the discount rate used by the lessee in calculating lease-related expenses for an accounting period. He concluded that lease-related expense in early years would increase with the discount rate and that the maximum discount rate was different for different lease lives.[16]

Baruch Lev and Aba Schwartz maintained, in 1971, that the disclosure of human capital values by business enterprises would provide users of financial statements with valuable information. They measured human capital by determining the present value of the remaining future earnings to the firm from employment of that individual.[17]

In 1976, Henry N. Amato, Evan E. Anderson, and David W. Harvey addressed the measurement and reporting of the costs associated with a warranty rebate program offered on repairable products. They took the position that rebate and evaluation costs should be discounted to their present value using the rate of return on investments with the same risks.[18]

In 1980 the American Institute of Certified Public Accountants (AICPA) released *Accounting for the Inability to Fully Recover the Carrying Amounts of Long Lived Assets.* Various measurements of assets were considered: one was the net present value of expected future cash flows. Those against reporting the inability to fully recover long-lived assets indicated several problems, including (1) inaccuracies in forecasting cash flows, (2) ascribing revenue to a particular long-lived asset, and (3) the subjectivity of the discount rate.[19]

Depreciable Assets

Two proposed methods of depreciation are based primarily on the notion that some rate of return should be realized on the net investment in fixed assets: the sinking fund and the annuity methods. While they have not been included as part of the AICPA's *Inventory of Generally Accepted Accounting Principals* (GAAP), they were first discussed by Pearcy Leake in 1912. He recognized that interest on capital should be considered a cost of production but did not think "that interest should be added to the provision for depreciation in commercial accounting."[20]

William A. Paton also examined these two interest-based depreciation methods in the 1943 edition of his *Accountant's Handbook.* He observed that interest is a factor in the cost of fixed assets and the revenue realized from the use of the fixed assets should reflect the interest earned on the remaining value of the investment.[21]

Maurice Moonitz and Louis H. Jordan reviewed the interest methods of depreciation in their 1963 book *Accounting: Analysis of Its Problems.* These authors recommended use of the annuity method to allocate depreciation.[22]

In 1975, *Accounting for Depreciable Assets,* Charles W. Lamden and his co-authors reviewed the use of interest methods of depreciation. They concluded that interest methods of depreciation are most appropriate when:

1. The net revenue contributions or operating efficiencies of an asset are indeterminable or, to the extent determinable, have to be constant or have to increase with the age of the asset.
2. The asset is used by an enterprise that is able to price its goods and services so as to obtain a fixed rate of return on its investment.
3. Other assets and related charges are expected to be constant or to decrease over the estimated life of the asset.[23]

Oil and Gas Reserves

In 1978, the Security and Exchange Commission (SEC) issued *Accounting Series, Release (ASR), no. 253*, which dealt with Reserve Recognition Accounting (RRA). *ASR no. 253*, which has since been suspended, required mandatory disclosure of the present value of estimated future net revenues from proven oil and gas reserves as supplementary information. The integrity of the estimates required by RRA in computing discounted cash flows from future oil and gas production was strongly challenged by practicing accountants.

In 1979, Yuji Ijiri reviewed a symposium on oil and gas accounting. According to him, the basic controversy at the symposium centered around the method of costing and valuing oil and gas reserves. While many of the participants did not appear to be ready to accept a value-based balance sheet, there seemed to be strong support for supplementary disclosure of reserve values.[24]

Also in 1979, Joseph E. Connor reported on a study by Price Waterhouse on the procedures to be used and related problems with RRA. Some of its conclusions were:

1. The theoretical viability of RRA is critically impaired by the reality of the inherent imprecision of the initial estimates of reserves and of future development and production activities.
2. RRA will not facilitate the development of a reliable energy data base.
3. RRA valuation and discounting problems with foreign reserves appear surmountable.[25]

In a 1983 paper, Timothy R. Bell reported on the results of his study of the stock market's reaction to the initial disclosure of RRA information. He found significant evidence of widespread reaction by the stock market, indicating that the RRA data conveyed new and useful information. Similarly, in 1984, Bala G. Dharan found that the stock market's reactions indicated that RRA data were useful, even though RRA data convey only limited information when considered as increments to other RRA data.[26]

Also in 1984, S. Basu and B. E. Lynn reviewed the present value disclosure required in a supplementary unaudited statement of oil and gas producers. They found that information about discounted values could provide a better estimate of the firm's worth than conservative historical cost figures.[27]

In 1987, Trevor S. Harris and James A. Ohlson examined the accounting disclosures and the market's valuation of oil and gas properties. The existence of several valuation measures for oil and gas properties raised the issue of how these valuation measures related to the market value of the oil and gas properties. Analysis of the data supported the hypothesis that book values are relevant and that book values are no less important than measures of present value.[28]

Examples of Discounting Problems in Accounting Standards

There has not been a comprehensive guide to the use of discounting in financial reporting. In chapter 3, we reviewed attempts to provide guidance to the process of setting standards, noting that these attempts to guide standard setting consistently recognized a role for present value in financial reporting, while none provided a comprehensive guide to its use. In chapter 4, we reviewed discounting in accounting standards, a review that indicated that the use of discounting specifically included in accounting standards is not consistent. Some examples of the problems encountered in using the standards for financial reporting of discounting are discussed in this section.

Bonds Payable

Accounting Research Bulletin, No. 2, issued by the AICPA, was the first standard that resulted in the use of discounting in financial reporting. This standard required that a discount on bonds payable be treated as part of the cost of borrowed money and that this cost should be distributed systematically over the term of the issue. The effect was to present bonds payable at present value at the date of issue.[29] Neither the guidance to standard setting nor subsequent standards themselves have addressed the issues involved in the recognition of present value after the date of the original recognition of a bond liability.

In 1983, Donald S. Shannon and William Stevens contended that not recognizing the market value of the bond subsequent to the date of issue results in not recognizing fair value. One of the problems that results from not recognizing fair value is that an early extinguishment of debt results in recognizing an extraordinary gain or loss. They contended that to recognize fair value prior to retirement would remove a serious motivational conflict from management when the debt is extinguished early.[30]

Another paper in 1983 observed a need for current value information about long-term debt in analyzing financial statements. The authors demonstrated an approach to revaluation of long-term debt using present value calculations, and showed the effect of this revaluation on the capital position.[31]

Interest on Receivables and Payables

Interest on receivables and payables is related to the proper reporting of bonds payable. The proper reporting of interest on receivables and payables was addressed in the Accounting Principles Board's (APB) *Opinion no. 21*.[32] This standard was a limited effort to address present value in accounting standards in a general manner, and there were many instances in which it did not apply. When it does apply, it applies to the date of the original transaction and not to subsequent changes in present value.

Opinion no. 21 states that the appropriate interest rate should be determined by considering factors such as the credit standing of the issuer, collateral, and payment terms. Subsequent standards have frequently referred to this one as a reference in determining the proper interest rate to be used for discounting.

Accounting for Troubled Debt Restructurings

Statement of Financial Accounting Standards *no. 15: Accounting by Debtors and Creditors for Troubled Debt Restructurings* was issued to clarify the accounting for a troubled debt restructuring. A troubled debt restructuring occurs when "the creditor for economic or legal reasons related to the debtor's financial difficulties grants a concession to the debtor that it would not otherwise consider."[33]

In this *Statement*, present value was not recognized, and precluded the recognition of the change in value that is inherent in a troubled debt restructuring. Troubled debt restructuring would generally result in an unrecognized gain to the debtor and an unrecognized loss to the creditor on the basis of a computation that uses projected gross cash flow resulting from the debt. Any unrecognized gains or losses are measured as the difference between the book value of the obligation immediately prior to restructuring and the undiscounted total future cash flows required after restructuring. Therefore, the debtor has a gain and the creditor has a loss if the carrying amount of the obligation is greater than the total future cash flows. If the total projected future cash flows are more than the book value, no gain or loss is recognized.

Thus, this standard did not use present value although the circumstance appeared to call for its use. In a troubled debt restructuring we know the projected cash flow and its timing. The only estimate required is the proper discount rate that reflects the risk of non-payment.

The Proper Interest Rate

One of the major decisions entailed in discounting is the interest rate to use; involved is an estimate of the opportunity cost of the money. While the amounts and time periods to be used in discounting can sometimes be reliably measured, in practice it is usually difficult to assess accurately the discount rate to be used. Standards that have included discounting have included a variety of directions on the determination of the interest rate. In exhibit 5-1 we have tabulated the bases for interest rates that have been used in past standards.

As indicated by this exhibit, there has been a wide variation in the prescribed discount rates. The difficulty of determining the appropriate rate most likely accounts for this variation. A brief review of the economic bases influencing the appropriate discount rate will help us to understand the difficulty.

Numerous economic theories of the time value of money have been advanced: the major ones are summarized in the Annotated Bibliography. However, for our present purpose, it is sufficient to say that, according to economic theory, the rate of interest i depends on the following factors which must be estimated in any determination of the appropriate rate of discount:

1. The rate of interest reflects the fact that the lender foregoes possession of the money in exchange for a promise of future possession of money—an amount that would include the amount loaned plus some compensation in the form of increased purchasing power for postponing its immediate consumption. This rate of interest is often known as the "real" (after adjustment for inflation) "riskless rate of return."

2. The lender must be compensated for any decline in purchasing power because of inflation during the period of the loan. If the interest rate is set prior to the end of the loan period, this inflationary change must be estimated. For cross-border lending, the charge for a decline in purchasing power must also include the effect of changing exchange rates.

EXHIBIT 5-1 **Examples of Interest Rates Used in Standards for Discounting**

Standard	*Description of Interest Rates*
APB, *Opinion no. 5: Reporting of Leases in Financial Statements of Lessee*[34] "The property and the obligation should be stated in the balance sheet at an appropriate discounted amount of future payments under the lease"—par. 15.	No particular interest rate indicated
APB, *Opinion no. 16: Business Combinations*[35]	"The effective rate of current yield for an otherwise comparable security"—par. 72.
	"Receivables determined at appropriate current interest rates"—par. 88.
APB, *Opinion no. 21: Interest on Receivables and Payables*[36]	"The market rate of interest"—par. 9.
	"An applicable interest rate"—par. 10.
APB, *Opinion no. 31: Disclosure of Lease Commitments by Lessees*[37]	"Based on the interest rates implicit in the terms of the leases"—par. 11.
SFAS, no. 13: Accounting for Leases[38]	"Using the interest rate implicit in the lease"; "using his incremental borrowing rate"—par. 7.
SFAS, no. 15: Accounting by Debtors and Creditors for Troubled Debt Restructurings[39]	"In substance the 'interest' rate method prescribed by paragraph 15 of APB *Opinion no. 21*"—par 16.
SFAS, no. 28: Accounting for Sales with Leasebacks[40]	"Using the interest rate that would be used to apply the 90 percent recovery criterion of paragraph 7? [of *SFAS*, no. 13]"—par 3.
SFAS, no. 33: Financial Reporting and Changing Prices[41]	"At an appropriate discount rate that allows for the risk of the activities concerned"—par. 63.
SFAS, no 47: Disclosure of Long-Term Obligations[42]	"The effective initial interest rate of the borrowings. . . . If not, the discount rate shall be the purchaser's incremental borrowing rate"—par 8.
SFAS, no. 53: Financial Reporting by Produces and Distributors of Motion Picture Films[43]	"Computed in accordance with the provisions of APB *Opinion* no. 21"—par. 9
SFAS, no.63: Financial Reporting by Broadcasters[44]	"Calculated in accordance with the provisions of APB *Opinion* no. 21"—par. 4.

Standard	*Description of Interest Rates*
SFAS, no.65: Accounting for Certain Mortgage Banking Activities[45]	"Based on an appropriate interest rate"—par. 11
SFAS, no.66: Accounting for Sales of Real Estate[46]	"Appropriate long-term interest rate"—par. 18
	"Paragraphs 13 and 14 of APB *Opinion no. 21: Interest on Receivables and Payables,* provide criteria for selecting an appropriate rate for present-value"—par. 23.
SFAS, no.69: Disclosures about Oil and Gas Producing Activities[47]	"Using a discount rate of 10 percent a year"—par. 30.
SFAS, no.87: Employers' Accounting for Pensions[48]	"The rates at which the pension benefits could be effectively settled"—par. 44.
SFAS, Interpretation no. 9: Applying APB Opinion nos. 16 & 17 When a S & L Asso. or a Similar Institution Is Acquired by the Purchase Method[49]	"At appropriate current interest rates"—par. 5
	"At appropriate current interest rates . . . using prevailing interest rates of similar liabilities at the acquisition date"—par. 7.

Notes: A number of other standards address present value but do not include a description of the interest rate to be used.

Numbered notes are included in "Notes", which follow.

3. Lenders must also be compensated for the risk of loss resulting from possible default by the borrower. Naturally, such risk and compensatory amount must be estimated prior to the end of the loan period. In cases of cross-border lending, such risks should also include default arising from governmental action that may be unrelated to the ability and willingness of the borrower to discharge the incurred obligation. In addition, a holder of an asset or a liability may face liquidation costs because of incomplete or inefficient markets. The amount of extra compensation related to the risks of default and liquidity is commonly known as the "risk premium."

Thus, the nominal interest rate—or the time value of money or the rate of discount—reflects at least three difficult-to-assess factors: a real riskless rate of return for foregoing present consumption, the estimated rate of inflation, and the amount needed to compensate for the risks of possible losses related the to borrower's default or the lack of liquidity. This can *be*expressed algebraically as:

$$1+i = (1+r)(1+f)(1+p)$$

where

i = the nominal interest rate
r = the real riskless rate of return
f = the expected inflation, or rate of loss of purchasing power
p = the risk premium

Simplifying the above expression, one obtains:

$$i = r + f + p + rf + rp + fp + rfp$$

Only when r, f, and p are all small numbers can the product terms be ignored and the relationship simplified to the commonly known one:

$$i = r + f + p$$

Even when an objective value for the riskless discount rate is obtainable from well-functioning and efficient capital markets, the adjustment for risk preference must be evaluated. It is often especially difficult to achieve comparability and verifiability of the estimates of the risk-adjustment component of the discount rate that are suitable for a specific financial accounting application.

Conclusions

This chapter is a brief review of some of the problems encountered in the use of discounting in financial accounting. Further research is needed to develop comprehensive review both of the problems and the inconsistencies in the use of concepts of present value in financial reporting standards and practices.

Notes

1. Thomas Hill, "Some Arguments against the Inter–Period Allocation of Income Taxes," *Accounting Review* 32, no. 3 (July 1957): 357–362.
2. Hugo Nurnberg, "Discounting Deferred Tax Liabilities," *Accounting Review* 47, no. 4 (October 1972): 655–65.

3. Edward E. Williams and M. Chapman Findlay III, "Discounting Deferred Taxes Liabilities: Some Clarifying Comments," *Journal of Business Finance and Accounting* 2, no. 1 (Spring 1975): 121–33.

4. Stephen L. Meyers, "An Examination of the Relationship between Interperiod Tax Allocation and Present–Value Depreciation," *Accounting Review* 48, no. 1 (January 1973): 44–49.

5. Homer A. Black, *Interperiod Allocation of Corporate Income Taxes: Accounting Research Study*, no.9 (New York, [AICPA] American Institute of Certified Public Accountants, 1966); James E. Wheeler and Willard H. Galliart, *An Appraisal of Interperiod Income Tax Allocation* (Morristown, N.J: Financial Executives Research Foundation, 1974).

6. Harry I. Wolk and Michael G. Tearney, "Discounting Deferred Tax Liabilities: Review and Analysis," *Journal of Business Finance & Accounting* 7, no. 1 (Spring 1980): 119–33.

7. Kenneth Lemke and Paul R. Graul, "Deferred Taxes: An 'Explicit Cost' Solution to the Discounting Problem," *Accounting & Business Research* no. 3 (Autumn 1981): 309–15.

8. James O. Stepp, "Deferred Taxes: The Discounting Controversy," *Journal of Accountancy*, November 1985: 98–108.

9. M. C. Findlay and E. E. Williams, "Opportunity Cost, Discounting and Deferred Tax Liabilities: A Final Note," *Journal of Business Finance & Accounting* 12, no. 2 (Summer 1985): 183–85.

10. Sudro Brown and Jeffrey Lippitt, " Are Deferred Taxes Discountable?" *Journal of Business Finance & Accounting* 14, no. 1 (Spring 1987): 121–31, F. Rayburn, "A Chronological Review of the Authoritative Literature on Interperiod Tax Allocation: 1940–1985," *Accounting Historians Journal*, Fall 1986, 89–108.

11. Richard A. Ippolito, "The Economic Burden of Corporate Pension Liabilities," *Financial Analysts Journal*, January–February 1986, 22–34.

12. John Maher, "Pension Obligations and the Bond Credit Market: An Empirical Analysis of Accounting Numbers," *Accounting Review* 62, no. 4 (October 1987): 785–98.

13. *Financial Accounting Standards Board (SAFB), Statement of Financial Accounting Standards (SFAS), no. 87: Employers Accounting for Pensions* (Stamford, Conn: FASB), 1985; Barnet Berin, William Mercer, and Dale

Gerboth, "Is FAS 87 Workable? No," *Financial Executive*, September–October 1987, 18–22; Gerald I. White, " Is FAS 87 Workable? Yes," *Financial Executive*, September–October 1987): 19–24.

14. Nancy Connors, "Pension Accounting Revisited: Facing Up to FASB 87," *CFO*, October 1987, 60–66; Joseph C. Rue and David E. Tosh, "Continuing Unresolved Issues of Pension Accounting," *Accounting Horizons*, December 1987, 21–27.

15. William J. Morris and Bernard A. Coda, "Valuation of Equity Securities," *Journal of Accountancy*, January 1973, 48–54.

16. Arthur R. Wyatt, "Leases Should Be Capitalized," *CPA Journal*, September 1974, 35–38; Gadis J. Dillon, "The Discount Rate and Lease–Related Expense," *CPA Journal*, November 1979, 37–40.

17. Baruch Lev and Aba Schwartz, "On the Use of the Economic Concept of Human Capital in Financial Statements," *Accounting Review* 46 no. 1 (January 1971): 103–12.

18. Henry N. Amato, Evan E. Anderson and David W. Harvey, "A General Model of Future Period Warranty Costs," *Accounting Review* 51, no. 4 (October 1976): 854–62.

19. Task Force on Impairment of Value, Accounting Standards Division, AICPA *Issues Paper, 83-2: Accounting for the Inability to Fully Recover the Carrying Amounts of Long Lived Assets* (New York: AICPA, 1980).

20. Paul Grady, *Inventory of Generally Accepted Accounting Principles: [ARS] Accounting Research Study; no. 7* (New York: AICPA, 1965); Pearcy D. Leake, *Depreciation and Wasting Assets and Their Treatment in Computing Annual Profit and Loss* (London: Henry Goode & Son, 1912), 66.

21. William A. Paton, *Accountant's Handbook*, 3d ed. (New York: Ronald Press, 1943).

22. Maurice Moonitz and Louis H. Jordan, *Accounting: An Analysis of Its Problems*, (New York: Holt, Rinehart & Winston, 1963), 393.

23. Charles W. Lamden, Dale L. Gerboth and Thomas W. McRae, *Accounting Research Monograph no. 1: Accounting for Depreciable Assets* (New York: AICPA, 1975): 102.

24. Yuji Ijiri, "Oil and Gas Accounting: Turbulence in Financial Accounting," *Financial Executive*, August 1979, 18–26.

25. Joseph E. Connor, "Reserve Recognition Accounting: Fact or Fiction?" *Journal of Accountancy*, September 1979, 92–99.

26. Timothy B. Bell, "Market Reaction to Reserve Recognition Accounting," *Journal of Accounting Research*, Spring 1983, 1–17; Bala G. Dharan, "Expectation Models and Potential Information Content of Oil and Gas Reserve Value Disclosures," *Accounting Review*, April 1984, 199–217.

27. S. Basu and B. E. Lynn, "Discounted Cash–Flow Requirements in the Oil and Gas Industry," *Cost and Management*, November–December 1984, 15–25.

28. Trevor S. Harris and James A. Ohlson, "Accounting Disclosures and the Market's Valuation of Oil and Gas Properties," *Accounting Review* 62, no. 4 (October 1987): 651–70.

29. AICPA, *Accounting Research Bulletin, no. 2: Unamortized Discount and Redemption Premium on Bonds Refunded* (New York: AICPA, 1939).

30. Donald S. Shannon and William Stevens, "How Debt Refunding Can Cause Decision Conflicts," *Management Accounting*, December 1983, 40–44.

31. Fred A. Jacobs, Larry H. Beard, and A. L. Hartgrave, "Distortion of Financial Statements Inflations Impact on Long-Term Debt," *Credit & Financial Management*, February 1983, 15–33.

32. Accounting Principles Board, (APB), *Opinion no. 21: Interest on Receivables and Payables* (New York: AICPA, 1971).

33. FASB, SFAS no. 15, *Accounting by Debtors and Creditors for Troubled Debt Restructurings*, Statement of Financial Accounting Standards (Stamford, Conn.: FASB, 1977), par. 1.

34. New York: AICPA, 1964.

35. Idem, 1970.

36. Idem, 1971.

37. Idem, 1973.

38. FASB (FASB: Stamford, Conn., 1976).

39. Idem, 1977.

40. Idem, 1979.

41. Idem, 1979.

42. Idem, 1981.
43. Idem, 1981.
44. Idem, 1982
45. Idem, 1982.
46. Idem, 1982.
47. Idem, 1982.
48. Idem, 1985.
49. Idem, 1976.

6
Conclusions

This study is a review of the literature on the use of discounting and the concepts of present value in financial accounting. We find that this literature has evolved to cover a very broad array of issues and positions, ranging from highly theoretical discourses to very practical discussions about application in specific situations. Generally, the literature provides support for the use of discounting in financial accounting, however, there is some opposition to its use in specific areas.

Summary

Our review of the literature found that discounting can be used in three areas of accounting. First, it can be used to assess fair value in initial recognition. Second, it can be used for subsequent revaluation. Third, it can be used to amortize an asset or liability. However, discounting is not being applied uniformly to similar resources and obligations of a firm and may not be consistently reported in financial statements.

We find that the use of discounting techniques in financial accounting is complicated by the conflict between the resulting increase in relevance and the resulting uncertainties that reduce its reliability or verifiability. Discounting also raises issues about the comparability and consistency of the resulting data.

Areas of Possible Future Research

Additional research is needed to assess the use of discounting in the many areas of accounting where it is used inconsistently. Examples of areas of inconsistencies in the use of discounting follow:

1. Pension obligations are discounted in the accounting process and interest as such obligations mature is reported as a portion of pension costs, whereas lease obligations are discounted to present value and the interest as these obligations mature is reported as interest expense. Thus, the cost of changing interest rates is classified in two different reporting categories. In both cases, the interest rate used remains a very important influence on reported values, especially since pension obligations (and some leases) are long term.

2. Problems of the impairment of value of fixed assets generally exclude consideration of the present value of cash flow and deal only in nominal dollars, whereas measurement of long-term monetary assets on a nondiscounted basis is appropriate only when they bear a reasonable rate of interest. Some perceive that practice is changing when writedowns are due to an impairment of value. Some of these writedowns are based on computations incorporating discounting, while others either ignore discounting or are based on methods that do not rely on discounting. As a result, some have asked for guidance from the Financial Accounting Standards Board (FASB), including AcSEC, which sent the FASB an issues paper, "Accounting for the Inability to Fully Recover the Carrying Amounts of Long Lived Assets."[1] Any final pronouncement on the appropriate manner in which to calculate a writedown due to impairment of asset value must address discounting.

3. The Accounting Principles Board's (APB) *Opinion no. 21* covers use of present value in valuing future contractual flows of cash. The American Institute of Certified Public Accountant's (AICPA), 1987 *Issues Paper number 87-2* similarly covers the use of the present value concept in valuing future non-contractual cash flows, but its conclusions have not yet been incorporated into an accounting standard.[2] In addition, APB's *Opinion no. 21* restricts the use of present value to receivables and short-term notes exceeding approximately one year. When interest rates are relatively high, the one-year guideline may be too long. Furthermore, if these accounts constitute a large enough proportion of a company's assets, their discounted value may have a material impact on income. And, since long-term notes and other monetary investments are valued in terms of their discounted value, the determination of the appropriate interest rate to use would also be important in these valuations.

4. Non-interest bearing borrowings are required to be reflected at a discounted amount, whereas deferred income taxes are not so discounted.

The lack of discounting of deferred taxes can be important because of the potential amount of deferred taxes and the relatively long time period.

5. The measurement and reporting of oil and gas reserves is important for many firms. It needs to be explored whether the measurement of these reserves using discounting procedures would result in more useful financial statements, and whether such measures should be disclosed in financial statements, footnotes, or as supplementary information.

6. Under current Generally Accepted Accounting Principles, troubled debt restructuring generally result in an unrecognized gain to the debtor and an unrecognized loss to the creditor. This is because the projected gross cash flow on the debt is compared with the book value at the time of restructuring. In a troubled debt restructuring we know the projected cash flow and the timing of the cash flow. However, an estimate of the discount rate that reflects the risk of non-payment is required. Research is needed to determine the appropriate discount rate.

7. Several other future liabilities are also not discounted in practice. Examples are warranties, unearned revenue, and provisions for compensated absences. Research is needed to develop procedures for applying present value to these problems.

These are just some examples of areas of financial accounting where the use of discounting is important but unclear. Because of the uncertain nature of measures based on discounted present values, it is possible to arrive at different conclusions about the discounting of cash flow in any given area of financial accounting. Empirical research into each specific application is needed to resolve the conflict between the increase in relevance and usefulness and the decrease in verifiability and reliability. Considerable analysis and judgment regarding the costs and benefits of present value techniques in accounting measurement are also required. Research is also needed to determine whether the informational content of financial statements would be improved if discounting were more broadly and uniformly applied and, if so, whether the improvement would justify the cost.

Conclusions

Our review of the literature indicates that discounting in financial accounting is recommended by some writers in some situations while others have opposed its use in the same situation. The controversy about the usefulness of discounting and present value in financial accounting can best be understood in the context of the tradeoffs involved. In each application, gains in the relevance of accounting information have to be balanced by the resulting decline in the reliability of the accounting measures. Research is necessary to assess when the advantages exceed the cost of using less reliable measures.

In sum, while the current use of discounting in financial accounting is plagued by many inconsistencies, the literature indicates substantial support for its use in financial accounting. The use of discounting offers improvements in the relevance and the usefulness of financial reporting and accounting information.

Notes

1. Task force on Impairment of Value, Accounting Standards Division, American Institute of Certified Public Accountants (AICPA), I*ssues Paper 83-2: Accounting for the Inability to Fully Recover the Carrying Amounts of Long Lived Assets*, 1983, New York, N.Y.

2. Task Force on Discounting Applications, Accounting Standards Division, American Institute of Certified Public Accountants (AICPA), *Issues Paper 87-2: The Use of Discounting In Financial Reporting for Monetary Items With Uncertain Terms Other than those Covered by Existing Authorative Literature*, 1987, New York, N.Y.

Selected Annotated Bibliography

Articles

Aggarwal, Raj. "The Translation Problem in International Accounting: Insights for Financial Management." *Management International Review* 15, nos. 2–3, (1975): 67–79.

This paper presented a management framework for analyzing translation procedures. The author contended that, for financial statements to reflect accurately the value of balance sheet items after changes in the exchange rate, the translation procedure used must be based on an estimate of how the present value of the cash flow associated with that item will change with the exchange rate if it is to satisfy the financial management and planning needs of the multinational firm.

Amato, Henry N., Evan E. Anderson, and David W. Harvey, "A General Model of Future Period Warranty Costs." *Accounting Review* 51, no. 4 (October 1976): 854–62.

The authors addressed the measurement and reporting of costs associated with a warranty rebate program offered on repairable products and took the position that rebate and evaluation costs should be discounted to their present values, using the opportunity rate of return.

Anthony, Robert N. "Equity Interest: Its Time Has Come." *Journal of Accountancy*, December 1982: 76–93.

For a meaningful balance sheet, Anthony proposed a full recognition of the cost of equity interest. This would capitalize the cost of equity financing, the interest on plant and equipment during construction, and the interest on inventory and other current assets while they are held.

Anton, Hector R. "Accounting for Bond Liabilities." *Journal of Accountancy*, September 1956: 53–56.

Anton noted that bond transactions involve two liabilities: one, the promise to pay a certain amount at the maturity date, and the other a promise to pay interest. The position was taken that these liabilities should be presented at their discounted amount on the date of issue. This would result in the proper disclosure and one consistent method of presentation, rather than three bond situations: bonds issued at face, bonds issued at a discount, bonds issued at a premium. An example in the paper follows:

Long-term liabilities	
Bonds payable - principal (Face amount, $100,000.00 maturing January 1, 2006)	$ 8,464.73
Bonds payable - interest* (Semi-annual payment, $1,500.00	54,921.16
Total bond liability	$63,385.89

**Note:* It may be desirable to classify current installments due as current liabilities.

Ashton, R. K. "Asset Valuation and Imperfect Markets: An Extension." *Accounting & Business* Research, no. 1 (Spring 1985): 123–27.

This author "examines whether and under what conditions the use of replacement cost–net realizable value as valuation bases in financial reports will provide a robust proxy of an asset's expected present value where market imperfections are present in the final goods market." It was concluded that under certain assumptions and circumstances the replacement cost–net realizable value and the present value method would produce close results.

Barnea, Amir, and Harold Bierman, Jr. "Cash Flow Valuation and Depreciation." *Accounting & Business Research*, no. 2 (Summer 1974): 193–96.

Three alternative concepts of asset valuation were considered: replacement cost, present value, and resale value. The authors argued that all three measures have relevance, but that it is useful to report separately the value in use by a specific form as distinct from the market measures of value.

Basu, S., and B. E. Lynn, "Discounted Cash-Flow Requirements in the Oil Gas Industry." *Cost & Management*, November–December, 1984: 15–25.

The Securities and Exchange Commission (SEC) issued *Accounting Series Release (ASR) 269: Oil and Gas Producers, Supplemental Disclosures on the Basis of Reserve Recognition Accounting*, September 1979, and *ASR 289*, April 1981. The Financial Accounting Standards Board (FASB), issued *Statement of Financial Accounting Standards (SFAS), no. 69, Disclosures about Oil and Gas Producing Activities* in 1982. All three (*ASR 269 and 289 and SFAS no. 69*) recommended that present value based disclosures be used in a supplementary unaudited statement, and all *ASR's* and the *SFAS* used a standardized discount rate of 10 percent. The authors found that the discounted information can provide a better estimate of the firm's worth than the conservative historical cost figures. They recommended that the data be improved by an estimate of the "real" discount rate implicit in oil and gas returns.

Bedford, Norton M. "Accounting Measurements of Economic Concepts." *Journal of Accountancy*, May 1957: 52–62.

This examination of the divergencies between economists' concepts and accounting concepts concluded that when accountants have departed from economists' concepts, the departure was due to the use of more realistic concepts or to the existence of a measurement problem which made it necessary to use an approximation of the economists' concept.

Bell, Timothy Barnes. "Market Reaction to Reserve Recognition Accounting." *Journal of Accounting Research*, Spring 1983: 1–17.

In 1978 the SEC issued *ASR no. 253*, dealing with Reserve Recognition Acocunting (RRA). The integrity of the estimates required by RRA in computing discounted cash flows from oil and gas production was seriously challenged by the practicing accounting profession. The objective of this study was to ascertain the degree of the stock market's reaction to the initial disclosure of RRA information. Evidence of widespread reaction of stock prices to such disclosures would indicate that the data are useful, even though they may be imprecise. Consistent results were obtained in several tests, indicating that the stock market did react to RRA disclosures which some parties regarded as too imprecise to be useful.

Berin, Barnet N., William M. Merrer, and Dale Gerboth. "Is FAS 87 Workable?" *Financial Executive*, September–October 1987: 18–24.

This paper was set up in two parts. One presented the case that *SFAS no. 87* is not workable, while the other part presented the case that it is workable. One of the arguments against the *Standard* was the volatility it added to the income statement, due primarily to the requirements for choosing the interest rate for discounting purposes. The cost calculation is very sensitive to changes in the discount rate. It was also argued that the discount rate recommended was not relevant. The argument favoring the *Standard* was that the volatility is overemphasized because the *Standard* has several mechanisms to limit it.

Bierman, Jr., Harold. "Discounted Cash Flows, Price Level Adjustments and Expectations." *Accounting Review* 46, no. 4 (October 1971): 693–99.

One of the objectives of this paper was to present an example of how the concept of discounted cash flow may be used to better understand the application of accounting techniques to the reporting of economic events. It did this in a setting of accounting for long-lived assets during a period of changing price levels.

———. (1972), "Discounted Cash Flows, Price Level Adjustments and Expectations: A Reply." *Accounting Review* 47, no.3 (July 1972): 589–90.

Willis Greer had commented on an article by Harold Bierman entitled "Discounted Cash Flows, Price Level Adjustments and Expectations." He had commented that there were two errors in Bierman's paper. Bierman replied in this paper that his paper was not in error, but he acknowledged Greer's comments as important extensions of the paper.

———. "Discounted Cash Flows, Price Level Adjustments and Expectations: A Reply." *Accounting Review* 47, no. 4 (October 1972): 799–800.

Thomas Dyckman and Willis Greer had commented on an article by Harold Bierman entitled "Discounted Cash Flows, Price Level Adjustments and Expectations." In this paper Bierman replied that there were no errors in his article, but that there were opportunities for extension. He acknowledged that both Dyckman and Greer had usefully extended the model of his article.

Bodenhorn, Diran. "Balance Sheet Items as the Present Value of Future Cash Flows." *Journal of Business, Finance, & Accounting* 11, no. 4 (Winter 1984): 493–510.

The purpose of the paper was to determine what a balance sheet would look like if it were based on potential cash flow (potential service), and what problems would be involved in its construction. The author was trying to prove that a balance sheet can be based on potential cash flow. He concluded that using this approach would present the balance sheet in "net value" of its items, or contra-values within.

Brief, Richard P., and Joel Owen. "Present Value Models and the Multi-Asset Problem." *Accounting Review* 48, no. 4 (October 1973): 690–95.

This paper illustrated the use of the internal rate of return for both the multi-asset problem and revenue separability, using the estimation theory. The author concluded that the internal rate of return is best applied to a firm and is not a single-asset model.

———. "Present Value Models and the Multi-Asset Problem: A Reply." *Accounting Review* 48, no. 4 (October 1973): 819–21.

In this paper the authors responded to several questions raised about the paper described above. They contended that the basic issue in their paper concerned the problem of interpreting aggregate data for the firm. They replied that they demonstrated a limitation of single-asset internal rate of return models and showed that this difficulty can be avoided by defining the internal rate of return as a concept applicable to the whole firm.

Bromwich, Michael. "Asset Valuation with Imperfect Markets." *Accounting & Business Research*, no. 3 (Autumn 1975); 242–53.

The author thought that the use of present value as the valuation system in accounting reports was normally held to be impractical and that it was therefore relegated to aiding in the selection of more acceptable valuation systems, such as replacement cost or net realizable value. He concluded that neither replacement cost nor net realizable value are reliable surrogates for present value.

———. "The Use of Present Value Valuation Models in Published Accounting Reports." Accounting Review 52, no. 3, (July 1977): 587–95.

The author argued that the present value model can serve as an ideal valuation model only under fairly restrictive conditions and that a single present value estimate could not serve all investors under all circumstances. This argument suggests that efforts be addressed to disclosing the fundamental variables that underlie such calculations of present value.

Brown, Sudro, and Jeffrey Lippitt. "Are Deferred Taxes Discountable?" *Journal of Business Finance & Accounting* 14, no. 1 (Spring 1987): 121–31.

This paper includes a summary of past articles addressing discounting of deferred taxes. Its purpose was to continue the examination of the nature of deferred taxes and the appropriateness of using present value for deferred taxes. The analysis centered on the procedures for applying the discount rate and on a numerical example.

Chambers, R. J. "Measurement in Accounting." *Journal of Accounting Research* 3, no. 1 (Spring 1965): 32–62.

Chambers held that the properties of an accounting system should be those of measurement systems generally. The products of such a system would have the qualities of relevance, neutrality, correspondence, communicability, and objectivity.

———. "Measures and Values: A Reply to Professor Staubus." *Accounting Review* 43, no. 2 (April 1968): 239–47.

This paper is a reply to George Staubus's 1967 article "Current Cash Equivalent for Assets: A Dissent," qv. Staubus believed that current cash equivalent represents a second-best value, while Chambers expounded on its use.

———. "Present Value Accounting." *Accountant*, April 16, 1970: 551–55.

In this paper, Chambers took a position against the use of present value in financial accounting, arguing that it did not survey information about the magnitude of the resources available to a firm at any time and did not indicate which of the alternatives was financially possible. He contended that present value accounting was essentially static, providing no informational base.

———. "Asset Measurement and Valuation." *Cost & Management*, March–April 1971: 30–35.

In this paper, the author took issue with Richard Mattessich's 1970 article "On the Perennial Misunderstanding of Asset Measurement by Means of Present Values," qv. According to Chambers, present values were as necessary in decision making as measurements, but the two were not the same. Therefore, only confusion could result from using "measurement" in reports of both values.

———. "Income and Capital: Fisher's Legacy." *Journal of Accounting Research* 9, no. 1 (Spring 1971): 137–49.

Irving Fisher's book *The Nature of Capital and Income* (qv.) is often credited with introducing present value to economists. John Canning, an accountant, drew heavily on Fisher's work when he authored *The Economics of Accountancy* (qv.) in the late 1920s. Canning is generally credited with introducing present value to accounting. In this article, Chambers reviewed Fisher's work. He noted that some parts of Fisher's work supported the view that balance sheet values of assets should properly be market values or prices, but that other parts supported the view that balance sheet values should be present values of the expected net proceeds of assets.

———. "Measurement and Valuation, Again." *Cost and Management*, July–August 1971: 12–17.

This paper is a reply to Richard Mattessich's "On Further Misunderstandings about Asset Measurement and Valuation: A Rejoinder to Chambers' Article," qv. Mattessich had taken the position that complementing market values by present values could aid in making practical decisions. Mattessich also regarded valuation as a kind of measurement. Chambers disagreed that valuation is a kind of measurement and with using present value as a form of measurement.

Connor, Joseph E. "Reserve Recognition Accounting: Fact or Fiction?" *Journal of Accountancy*, September 1979: 92–99.

This paper was a report of a study by Price Waterhouse on the procedure to be followed in RRA and the problems related to it. Some of the conclusions of this study were: (1) the theoretical viability of RRA is crucially impaired by the inherent imprecision of initial estimates of reserves and future development and production activities, (2) RRA does not facilitate the development of a reliable energy data base, and (3) RRA valuation and disclosure problems associated with foreign reserves appear surmountable.

Connors, Nancy. "Pension Accounting Revisited: Facing Up to FASB 87." *CFO,* October 1987: 60–66.

This paper reviews the Financial Accounting Standards Board's (FASB) *Statement no. 87,* which called for the present value of an employee's pension to be based on length of service and the distribution of this cost to be based on the actual value that the pension has in any given year of the employee's service. The standard also mandated a new way of determining interest rates that would be used as the discount rate. This standard could require companies to re-estimate future earnings on pension assets every year, depending on changes in interest rates.

Cook, John S., and Oscar J. Holzmann. "Current Cost and Present Value in Income Theory." *Accounting Review* 51, no. 4,(October 1976): 778–87.

The authors examined replacement cost income as an ideal surrogate measure of economic income for firms operating in perfectly competitive markets. They observed that a necessary condition is the presence of general equality between the market prices of assets and the expected present values of their future cash flows, and demonstrated that this condition may be expected.

Corbin, Donald A. "The Revolution in Accounting." *Accounting Review* 37, no. 4 (October 1962): 626–635.

The author noted that the economists' forward-looking approach, found in managerial accounting, was not widely adopted in financial accounting and claimed that the "revolution" involved a willingness to modify the historical cost and realization principles of accounting. Corbin also observed that Prof. John Canning, who was noted for his linking of accounting to economics, suggested that income be determined by directly valuing each asset and liability at the beginning and end of each accounting period.

Cramer, Joe J. "The Nature and Importance of Present Value in Financial Accounting." *Arthur Andersen Chronicle,* September 1977: 27–36.

The first of Cramer's three-part series in the *Arthur Andersen Chronicle,* it covered: (1) the nature of the principle of present value as it relates to financial accounting; (2) the objective of the study, identifying certain questions related to discounting and financial accounting; (3) an evaluation of the current status of discounting in financial accounting; and (4) an explanation of how a clear-cut classification of assets and liabilities helps determine the applicability of discounting to financial accounting in general. Cramer acknowledged that monetary and nonmonetary financial items are subject to different risks, but felt this was of less consequence than the fact that they are both financial in nature, which should be the dominating criterion.

———. "The Nature and Importance of Discounted Present Value in Financial Accounting and Reporting." *Arthur Andersen Chronicle*, September 1978: 46–56.

The second part of Joe Cramer's series focused on the role of discounting in accounting for financial assets and liabilities. He attempted to demonstrate that the same systematic set of procedures relevant to accounting for monetary items can be applied to nonmonetary financial assets and liabilities. Thus, he found discounting as useful in accounting for nonmonetary financial items as for monetary items.

———. "The Nature and Importance of Discounted Present Value Financial Accounting and Reporting." *Arthur Andersen Chronicle*, September 1979: 43–48.

The third part of Joe Cramer's series revealed that, because the value of operating assets is affected by all of the risks and uncertainties that characterize the earning process, direct discounting is of limited practical usefulness in accounting for them.

Craswell, A. T. "Surrogates in Accounting." *Abacus* 14 (June 1978): 81–93.

Craswell reviewed the place and use of surrogates in financial accounting theory. Surrogates are used in accounting, behavioral research, and accounting theory, giving rise to uncertainty about the generality of any conclusions that may be derived. He showed that the various valuation bases cannot be substituted for present values and justified as surrogates. Craswell concluded that historical cost, replacement cost, net realizable value, and present value are conceptually separate and distinct and therefore may not be interchanged in accounting theories.

Crossen, Cynthia. "New Accounting Rule May Affect Pensions of Millions of People." *Wall Street Journal*, (January 18, 1988): 11–12.

This article was a comment on the FASB's *Statement no. 87*. It noted that the expected liabilities must be recalculated annually, using market interest rates and that, as interest rates change, the pension liability will change, as will income.

Curley, Anthony, and Charles G. Carpenter. "Present Value Models and the Multi-Asset Problem: Comment." *Accounting Review* 48, no. 4 (October 1973): 812–15.

In a response to Brief and Owen's "Present Value Models and the Multi-Asset Problem," qv., the authors maintained that Brief and Owen's analysis was incomplete, and their conclusion therefore misleading. They argued that it is useful to consider the properties of an internal rate of return and, accordingly, the properties of the amortization model of the internal rate of return.

Dascher, P. E., V. C. Brenner, and J. J. Benjamin. "Present Value: A Review." *National Public Accountant* 20 (June 1975): 18–21.

This review of the basic techniques of using present value in financial accounting also presented the application of present value in selected accounting problems.

Davidson, Sidney. "Accelerated Depreciation and the Allocation of Income Taxes." *Accounting Review* 33, no. 2 (April 1958): 173–80.

In this argument against comprehensive tax allocation, it was contended that discounting of the deferral is required and that, if a reasonable discount rate is used, the present value of the deferred taxes would be relatively small.

Dewhirst, John F. "A Conceptual Approach to Pension Accounting." *Accounting Review,* April 1971: 365–373.

The author examined the conceptual soundness of cost methods as a basis for pension accounting. He discussed the appropriateness of three measures of the discount rate—estimated earnings rate, the long-run bond rate for the company, and the company's cost of capital— and favored the last measure as the most appropriate discount rate.

Dharan, Bala G. "Expectation Models and Potential Information Content of Oil and Gas Reserve Value Disclosures." *Accounting Review* April 1984: 199–217.

Dharan examined the potential informational content of oil and gas reserve value disclosure requirements mandated by RRA. He found strong linear relationships which imply that RRA signals may have potentially low incremental information content, in the sense that they may not have much incremental impact on observed security prices. Errors of prediction at the firm level were often large, implying the usefulness of RRA data in other contexts.

Dillon, Gadis J. "The Discount Rate and Lease-Related Expense." *CPA Journal* November 1979: 37–40.

This examination of the implication of estimating the discount rate used by the lessee in calculating lease-related expenses to be reported for an accounting period concluded that lease-related expense in early years would increase with increases in the discount rate up to a given rate. The maximum discount rate was found to be different for different lease lives.

Dollar, Cecil, Jr. "Measurement of Liabilities at Current Values." *National Public Accountant* 18 (January 1973): 24–25.

The writer recommended that liabilities should be measured at current values if assets are also measured at current values, indicating three advantages of using current values for liabilities: (1) it would be consistent with the measurement of assets, if assets are measured at current values; (2) it would base interest expense on the current market rate of interest; and (3) interest expense would reflect the cost that would have to be incurred in the current money market.

Dyckman, Thomas R. "Discounted Cash Flows, Price-Level Adjustments and Expectations: A Comment." *Accounting Review* 47, no. 4 (October 1972): 794–98.

A reply to a paper by Harold Bierman's 1971 paper, qv.

Edwards, J. R. and Alison Warman. "Discounted Cash Flow and Business Valuation in a Nineteenth Century Merger: A Note." *Accounting Historians Journal* 8, no. 2 (Fall 1981): 37–50.

The authors examined the use of discounted cash flow as a guide to the contracting parties in negotiating the price to be paid in a nineteenth-century merger. (In 1889 the Shelton Iron, Steel and Coal Company, Ltd. was incorporated to take over the assets and business activities of two existing companies.) The authors considered the mechanics of the valuation satisfactory, except for the use of a single year's results and a number of different interest rates depending on the nature and duration of estimated cash flows.

Findlay, M. Chapman, and Edward E. Williams. "Discounting Deferred Tax Liabilities: A Reply." *Journal of Business Finance & Accounting* 8, no. 4, (Autumn 1981): 593–597.

In reply to the comments made by Wolk and Tearney in 1980 (qv.), the authors disagreed about the appropriate discount rate to be used. They contended that the appropriate rate is the cost of equity, multiplied by 1, less the tax rate. Wolk and Tearney had contended that it should be a pre-tax debt rate augmented for additional risk.

———. "Opportunity Cost, Discounting, and Deferred Tax Liabilities: A Final Note." *Journal of Business Finance & Accounting* 12 , no. 2, (Summer 1985): 183–85.

This paper carried on the debate about whether deferred tax liabilities should be discounted at pre-tax or after-tax rates. The authors argued that the deferred tax liabilities should be discounted at after-tax rates, and concluded with a claimed proof of their position.

Finnerty, Joseph E., R. N. Fitzsimmons, and T. W. Oliver. "Lease Capitalization and Systematic Risk." *Accounting Review* 55, no. 4 (October 1980): 631–39.

In 1973, *ASR 147* was issued by the SEC. In 1976, FASB released *SFAS no. 13*. These documents were a major recognition of the capitalization of certain leases in financial reporting. Business leaders feared that a reduction in credit ratings and possibly higher interest rates would result from firms showing more "debt." The evidence in this paper indicated that no systematic effect on the market's assessment of risk was brought about by the change in these financial reporting requirements.

Forker, J. J. "Contract Value Accounting and the Monitoring of Managerial Performance: An Agency-Based Proposal." *Accounting & Business Research*, no. 1 (Spring 1984): 125–37.

Forker held that the present value method used by management is misleading and inappropriate, because the valuations are subjectively made by management, and that accountants do not have the competence to establish such values for the assets of a going concern.

Friedman, Laurence A. "What Is Current Value?" *CPA Journal*, November 1978: 24–28.

This discussion of some of the major valuation techniques which could be considered to provide measures of current value included replacement cost, exit value, and discounted cash flows. It was noted that all of the methods could be general price-level adjusted and that many considered the determination of future cash flows and the appropriate discount rate to be a completely subjective exercise.

Greer, Willis R. Jr. "Discounted Cash Flows, Price-Level Adjustments and Expectations: A Comment." *Accounting Review* 47, no. 3 (July 1972): 587–88.

In this paper, Willis Greer commented on Harold Bierman's 1971 article on discounted cash flows. qv. Greer claimed that Bierman made two errors in his analysis, each of which caused him to arrive at the same incorrect conclusion—that the predictability of inflation has a bearing on the value of price-level adjusted financial statements.

Harris, Trevor S., and James A. Ohlson. "Accounting Disclosures and the Market's Valuation of Oil and Gas Properties." *Accounting Review* 62, no. 4 (October 1987): 651–70.

The existence of several valuation measures of oil and gas properties raises the issue of how these valuation measures relate to the market value of the properties. This paper supported the hypothesis that the book values are relevant and no less important than the present value measures.

Henderson, Scott, and Graham Peirson. "A Note on the Current Cash Equivalent of Liabilities." *Abacus* 16 (June 1980): 61–66.

The authors reconsidered the appropriate method of measuring long-term liabilities under the continuously contemporary accounting system, and reviewed the methods advocated by R. J. Chambers, E. R. Iselin, R. Ma, and Lawrence Friedman. They concluded that, in spite of the merit of the proposals of both Ma and Iselin, the final results are not significantly different whether we measure long-term liabilities according to their current cash equivalent or market value. Further, they contend that Chambers' method of measuring long-term liabilities in a continuously contemporary accounting system is acceptable.

Hill, Thomas. "Some Arguments against the Interperiod Allocation of Income Taxes." *Accounting Review* 32, no. 3 (July 1957): 357–362.

Hill rebutted the arguments advanced by Maurice Moonitz in his April 1957 article in *Accounting Review* regarding the intra-period allocation of income taxes. Specifically, this author contested the realism of the Moonitz's assumption of a zero discount rate in valuing future tax payments and recommended using rates established in financial markets.

Holley, Charles L, and Douglas Ziegenfuss. "The Discounting Dilemma." The *CPA Journal*, October 1987, 100–101.

This article reviews the nature of the discounting dilemma in financial reporting. The authors suggest the development of a classification scheme that determines the receivables and payables to be discounted to overcome the current inconsistencies in the use of discounting.

Ijiri, Yuji. "Oil and Gas Accounting: Turbulence in Financial Reporting." *Financial Executive*, August 1979: 18–26.

This is a review of a symposium on oil and gas accounting in which the basic controversy centered on the methods of costing and valuing oil and gas reserves. Many of the participants did not appear to be ready to accept a value-based balance sheet, but supplemental disclosure of the present value of reserves as required by the SEC's *ASR no. 253* seemed to have strong support.

Ippolito, Richard A. "The Economic Burden of Corporate Pension Liabilities." *Financial Analysts Journal*, January–February 1986: 22–34.

Ippolito described the theory behind the valuation of pension liabilities and concluded that pension liabilities reported by firms fall short of their true liabilities. A portion of the paper was devoted to the proper discount rate to use when estimating pension liabilities: an approach considered was to assume that the stock market correctly calculates pension liabilities by using economic discount rates. According to this approach, the best guess of the discount rate used by the stock market to evaluate true pension liabilities is 2 percent per annum, since growth in pension liabilities due to inflation is expected to offset all but 2 percent of the average long-run growth of pension assets.

Jacobs, Fred A., Larry H. Beard, and A. L. Hartgraves. "Distortion of Financial Statements: Inflation's Impact on Long-Term Debt." *Credit & Financial Management*, February 1983: 15–33.

The authors took the position that there is a need for current value information about long-term debt because, if long-term debt is undervalued or overvalued, analysis of a financial statement can be distorted. Included is a demonstration of the revaluation of long-term debt using present value calculations and showing the effect of this revaluation on capital structure ratios.

Jones, Thomas W., and J. David Smith. "An Historical Perspective of Net Present Value and Equivalent Annual Cost." *Accounting Historians Journal* 9, no. 1 (Spring 1982): 103–10.

This paper traces the development of net present value and equivalent annual cost. Since the equivalent annual cost method appears in engineering literature and not in accounting literature, our comments are restricted to net present value. In 1887 an American civil engineer used net present value in a book on the locations of railways in an early attempt to apply present value to nonfinancial investments. The first reference to net present value in American economic literature was Irving Fisher's *The Rate of Interest* in 1907 (New York: Macmillian, 1907). In 1930, Eugene Grant discussed applications of present worth in his textbook, *Principles of Engineering Economy* (New York: Ronald Press, 1930). In 1938, J. F. Ebersole examined 757 cases on file at the Harvard School of Business in order to answer the question, "Is the interest rate an important influence in determining whether companies expand or contract their operations or plants?" (Harvard Business Review, Vol. XVII, no. 1 (Autumn 1938) 35-39). Ebersole concluded that the interest rate is not viewed as an important problem by business management. R. H. Parker attributed the lack of interest in net present value by accountants to their over-concern with historical cost. (Parker, R. H. *Management Accounting: An Historical Perspective* New York: M. Kelly, 1969). According to Jones and Smith, the first significant event appearing in accounting literature relating to capital budgeting and net present value was the 1960 publication of *The Capital Budgeting Decision* by Harold Bierman and S. Smidt (Bierman, H., Jr. and S. Smidt, *The Capital Budgeting Decision* 5th ed. New York: Macmillan, 1980). Although the authors intended to trace the development of net present value, their scope was actually limited to its use in managerial accounting.

Kollaritsch, Felix P. "Future Service Potential Value." *Journal of Accountancy*, February 1965: 57–62.

According to some accounting and economics literature, individual assets should be evaluated on the balance sheet at their future service potential value. This paper refuted that position and tried to show that the future service potential value is practically and theoretically unacceptable for accounting purposes.

Krebs, Eric H., and Joseph M. Jordan. "The Insurance Industry after the TRA." *Journal of Accountancy*, August 1987: 92–100.

For federal tax purposes, property and casualty insurance companies generally have been able to deduct the full amount of a loss currently even though that loss may not be paid for a number of years. The U.S. Congress believed that this accounting treatment did not properly reflect the time value of money and that, as a result, the current deduction for future loss payments was overstated. The Tax Reform Act of 1986 mandated that, in taxable years beginning after 1986, loss reserves must be discounted for tax purposes.

Larson, Kermit, and R. W. Schattke. "Current Cash Equivalents, Additivity, and Financial Action." *Accounting Review* 41, no. 4 (October 1966): 634–41.

This paper was an academic criticism of R. J. Chambers', *Accounting, Evaluation and Economic Behavior*, (Englewood Cliffs, N.J.: Prentice-Hall 1966). Chambers measured the factors involved in determining the financial position of a firm by current cash equivalent. Larson and Schattke claimed that current cash equivalent does not satisfy the requirement of additivity and indicated that discounted future service potential might be a possibility.

Langenderfer, Harold Q. "Accrued Post-Service Pension Costs Should Be Capitalized." *New York Certified Public Accountant*, February 1971: 137–54.

Langenderfer argued that there should be balance sheet recognition of pension liabilities. The paper was a response to *ASR no. 8* and the APB's *Opinion no. 8*, neither of which recommended balance sheet recognition of unfunded pension liabilities for past service.

Largay III, James A. Livingstone, and J. Leslie Livingstone. "Current Value Accounting Neglects Liabilities." *Financial Analysts Journal*, March–April 1978: 65–71.

The authors made the point that inflation accounting treats liabilities, in general, and long-term debt, in particular, inconsistently. The general price-level adjusted method deals with purchasing power changes in the principal of long-term debt but ignores both the market values and the current interest rate. The only method that adequately reports the impact of inflation on liabilities in general and long-term debt in particular is the combined replacement cost–general price-level adjusted method.

Lav, C. T. and M. Nelson. "A Note on Accounting for Leases." *Cost & Management*, March–April: 1981.

In January 1978, the Accounting Research Committee of the Canadian Institute of Chartered Accountants issued an exposure draft entitled "Accounting for Leases." This document was substantially similar to *Statement 13* previously issued by the FASB. Lev and Nelson identified a possible problem in interpreting parts of the Canadian standard. The problem was that the use of one discount rate (the implicit rate) to record the leased asset and obligation, and the use of another rate (the incremental borrowing rate) to amortize the obligation when the fair market value is less than the present value based on the incremental borrowing rate result in a residual debit in the lease obligation amount.

Lemke, Kenneth W. "Asset Valuation and Income Theory." *Accounting Review* 41, no. 1 (January 1966): 32–41.

Lemke reviewed asset valuation and income theory, noting that progress had been hindered by the interpretation of realization and the optimum accounting definition of asset values. He suggested that a compromise could be guided by the rule that each asset be valued according to the basis offering "sufficiently definite verifiable evidence" and yielding what he believed to be the closest approximation to the present value of the asset's future cash flows.

———. and Paul R. Graul "Deferred Taxes: An 'Explicit Cost' Solution to the Discounting Problem." *Accounting & Business Research*, no. 3 (Autumn 1981): 309–15.

After proposing a method of measuring deferred tax "liabilities" on a discounted present value basis and the discount rate to use, the authors concluded that the explicit rates of return should be used to compute the present value. This review of possible discount rates noted a widely held view that deferred taxes are an "interest-free loan" from the government, a view that has influenced several writers to conclude that a zero discount rate should be used. This would result in the deferred tax amount not being reduced.

Lev, Baruch, and Aba Schwartz "On the Use of the Economic Concept of Human Capital in Financial Statements." *Accounting Review* 46, no. 1 (January 1971: 103–12.

Irving Fisher defined capital as a source of income stream and its worth, described as the present value of future income discounted by a rate specific to the owner of the source. This definition does not distinguish between human and nonhuman capital. The authors maintained that the disclosure of human capital values by business enterprises would provide financial statement users with valuable information.

Maher, John J. "Pension Obligations and the Bond Credit Market: An Empirical Analysis of Accounting Numbers." *Accounting Review* 62, no. 4 (October 1987): 785–98.

The FASB requires corporations to make public disclosures regarding their defined benefit plans. Measurement of the future pension obligation is determined, in large part, by a company-chosen interest discount rate. The empirical analysis presented here provided evidence of whether a measure of pension obligations is considered in bond ratings. The results supported the idea that bond rating analysts were not being fooled by the use of high interest rates by some companies to minimize the reported pension obligation.

Martin, Carrick A. "The Current Cost of a Quoted Long-Term Liability." *Accounting & Business Research*, no. 2 (Summer 1983): 191–99.

The idea has been promoted by several writers that long-term liabilities should be reported at their current market values. Martin took the opposite view, which is that incorporation of current yields on liabilities would produce misleading information with respect to operating performance, financial stability and capital maintenance.

Mattessich, Richard. "On the Perennial Misunderstanding of Asset Measurement by Means of Present Value." *Cost & Management*, March–April 1970: 29–31.

Mattessich maintained that the accounting system ought to serve management as well as a legalistic objective and that dualistic or even multidimensional valuation is desirable and often indispensable. Thus, he felt that the controversy is not about whether assets should or should not be evaluated at present or other values, but about whether these values should be systematically incorporated in the accounting information system.

———. "On Further Misunderstandings about Asset Measurement and Valuation: A Rejoinder to Chambers' Article." *Cost & Management*, March–April 1971: 36–42.

This paper was a reply to R. J. Chambers, who had written an article about a previous article by Mattessich. Mattessich's earlier article promulgated the thesis that the acquisition cost basis or market basis should be complemented with present values to make accounting a tool for practical decisions. It was Mattessich's opinion that Chambers did not attack the essence of the article, but a peripheral issue regarding the definition of measurement. In particular, Chambers had disliked Mattessich's approach to valuation as a kind of measurement.

———. "Asset Measurement and Valuation: A Final Reply to Chambers." *Cost & Management*, July–August 1971: 18–23.

This paper was a rejoinder to Chambers' "Management and Valuation, Again," q.v., and a second rejoinder to the work of R. J. Chambers.

McIntyre, Edward V. "Present Value Depreciation and the Disaggregation Problem." *Accounting Review* 52, no. 1 (January 1977): 162–71.

Present value depreciation has been explored in the literature as a means of reconciling the conflict between the internal rate of return of capital in a budgeting model and the return on investment computed from financial statement data. The author concluded that various accounting methods can provide compatibility between the internal rate of return and the return on investment, but may yield individual account balances which lack economic substance.

Meyers, Stephen L. "An Examination of the Relationship between Interperiod Tax Allocation and Present-Value Depreciation." *Accounting Review* 48, no. 1 (January 1973): 44–49.

This analysis of the underlying conflict between present value depreciation and interperiod tax allocation suggests that present value depreciation be based on pre-tax benefits associated with depreciable assets. Meyers contended that such an approach would make the two concepts consistent with each other and with generally accepted accounting principles.

———. "Present Value Models and the Multi-Asset Problem: A Comment." *Accounting* Review 48, no. 4 (October 1973): 816–18.

This paper was a comment on Richard P. Brief and Joel Owens' "Present Value Models and the Multi-Asset Problem," qv. The purpose was to show that Brief and Owen's main conclusion, that the internal rate of return is essentially a firm model and not a single-asset model, is generally not valid.

Miller, Paul B. W., and David Messo. "Financial Accounting Measurement: Why Things May Not Be What They Seem to Be." *Financial Executive*, (December 1983): 28–35.

The authors argued that measurement in financial accounting should depend on the measurement of the relevant phenomenon by observing the magnitude of the relevant or substitute attribute. They further contended that the use of the present value of future benefits is an acceptable measurement, as it is based on the magnitude of a substitute attribute of the relevant phenomenon.

Mobley, Sybil C. "Measures of Income." *Accounting Review* 43, no. 2 (April 1968): 333–41.

Many authors have charged that the conventional income statement does not effectively report the full performance of the firm. Mobley suggested that a Statement of Financial Condition which includes a column headed "Costs" and another column headed "Projected Values" would improve financial reporting. The estimated values would be a measure of current financial worth and as such would be useful in supporting applications for loans, making interfirm comparisons, and in evaluating appreciation. The article did not directly address the use of present value, but present value could be one of the methods of determining "projected values."

Morris, William J. and Bernard A. Coda. "Valuation of Equity Securities." *Journal of Accountancy*, January 1973: 48–54.

This discussion was aimed at long-term investments in marketable equity securities by such entities as insurance companies and pension funds. The authors concluded that the use of current market value for long-term investments is not warranted and that the best available net realizable value is the accounting method with the minimum mean-square error from the present value of future cash proceeds.

Norris, Floyd. "The Great Accountancy Shoot-Out." *Barron's*, January 9, 1984: 44–47.

This review of pension accounting as of 1984 observed that pension accounting procedures were in a state of disarray as of 1984, when the FASB proposed a new standard for pension accounting that would be more uniform and would at least partially book pension liabilities.

Norstrom, Carl J. "The Deprival Value of Durable Assets." *Accounting & Business Research*, no. 3 (Autumn 1985): 265–70.

Accounting literature often uses three alternative general bases for the value of an asset: the replacement cost of the asset, the net realizable value of the asset, and the present value of the expected future net receipts from the asset. The purpose of this paper was to offer a reasonably unified treatment of the deprival value under conditions of certainty when the purchase price of the asset is higher than the net realizable value. Two numerical illustrations were used. One showed that it may be optimal to re-invest even if the present value of the existing asset is less than the purchase price of an asset of that age; the other showed that it may be optimal not to re-invest now even though the present value exceeds the purchase price.

Nurnberg, Hugo. "Present Value Depreciation and Income Tax Allocation." *Accounting Review* 43, no. 4 (October 1968): 719–29.

Definitive conclusions were not drawn in this review of present value depreciation and income tax allocation.

———. "Discounting Deferred Tax Liabilities." *Accounting Review* 47, no. 4 (October 1972): 655–65.

Nurnberg examined the arguments favoring and opposing accounting for deferred tax liabilities on a discounted basis, and also reviewed the rate of discount to be used for discounting. He noted that the balance sheet valuation of most liabilities approximate their present value, in current practice: other things being equal, the firm pays the same taxes with or without deferred taxes. A deferred tax liability represents an interest-free loan, and not to recognize interest is a departure from the usual concept of interest expense applicable to other liabilities. The conclusion was that deferred tax liabilities should be reported on a discounted basis but there was no conclusion about the appropriate rate of discount.

Parker, R. H. "Discounted Cash Flow in Historical Perspective." *Journal of Accounting Research* 6, no. 1 (Spring 1968): 58–71.

This survey of the development of discounted cash flow criteria of investment evaluation before 1950 indicated that discounted cash flow has its roots in compound interest, actuarial science, engineering, and capital theory. Although the net present value approach was applied to financial investments as early as 1582 and bond tables incorporating the equivalent of the internal rate of return were in use by the second half of the nineteenth century, it was not until the 1950s that interest in the use of discounted cash flow began to quicken. The author attributed this delay to the accounting profession's being more concerned with historical recording than with decision making and the fact that the education of accountants did not include much economic theory. The historical perspective provided by this paper did not include the use of discounting in financial accounting.

Paton, William. "Special Applications of Discounting." *Journal of Accountancy*, October 1928: 270–282.

This was a significant article on discounting in financial reporting because it was the first one to review the possible use of discounting in financial reporting and because it was an extensive review of the subject. Paton took the position that the province of discounting is a very narrow one and that discounting should apply in situations where future sums, payable in money or its equivalent, are assured by contract. He used several examples to illustrate the use of discounting in financial reporting.

———. "Valuation of the Business Enterprise." *Accounting Review* 11 no. 1, (March 1936): 390–91.

In an early recognition of present value, Paton, a highly respected academic accountant, recognized the income route to the valuation of the business enterprise. The income route accepted the view of many economists that present values of production facilities represent the sum of the values of the uses which may be expected to flow from such facilities or objects through the term of their effective existence, appropriately discounted to date.

Peasnell, K. V. "A Note on the Discounted Present Value Concept." *Accounting Review* 52 , no. 1 (January 1977): 186–89.

Peasnell recognized that the discounted present value concept plays an important part in accounting theory. But there are those who argue that the primary function of financial accounting is the assessment of achievements and that this indicates a need for ex post facto measures. Peasnell contended that accountants do not have a comparative advantage in the determination of discounted present value for investors and that this task should be left to the stock market.

———. "Some Formal Connections between Economic Values and Yields and Accounting Numbers." *Journal of Business, Finance & Accounting* 9, no. 3 (Autumn 1982): 361–81.

The purpose of this paper was to show how a firm's economic value and its economic yield can be derived from accounting numbers. Results indicating the mathematical connections between accounting and economic yields were developed.

Petersen, Russell J., and Thomas F. Keller. "Asset Valuation, Income Determination and Changing Prices." *Accounting Review* 47, no. 4 (October 1972): 801–5.

The author's purpose was to extend Bierman's analysis of estimating value using discounted cash flows, presented in "Discounted Cash Flows, Price-Level Adjustments and Expectations" qv.

Rayburn, F. "A Chronological Review of the Authoritative Literature on Interperiod Tax Allocation: 1940–85." *Accounting Historians Journal*, Fall 1986: 89–108.

This excellent review of the authoritative literature on interperiod tax allocation from 1940 to 1985 includes almost all of the alternatives proposed, including the use of discounting procedures. In summary, tax allocation has evolved from being required for specific transactions (Accounting Research Bulletin (ARB) 18, "Unamortized Discount and Redemption Premium on Bonds Refunded," 1942) to partial allocation using liability or net of tax methods (ARB 23, "Accounting for Income Taxes," 1944), to partial allocation using the liability method (ARB 42, "Emergency Facilities: Depreciation, Amortization, and Income Taxes," 1952), to the deferred method of comprehensive allocation (APB 11 "Accounting for Income Taxes," and APB 23, "Accounting for Income Taxes-Special Items," 1967 and 1972) to the liability method of comprehensive allocation with the exception of items in APB 23 (*SFAS no. 96*, 1987).

Rayburn, Frank R. "Discounting of Deferred Income Taxes: An Argument for Reconsideration." *Accounting Horizons*, March 1987, 43–49.

Rayburn reviews the literature over the period 1967-1987 on the issue of discounting of deferred taxes. He demonstrates that discounting of deferred taxes is theoretically consistent with measurement of liabilities. It is his opinion that the FASB's position that deferred taxes should not be discounted is conceptually irreconcilable.

Ronen, Joshua, and George H. Sorter. "Relevant Accounting." *Journal of Business*, April 1972: 258–82.

The authors presented a system, different from existing systems, of internal accounting reports designed to meet the need of investors to estimate future cash flows and their riskiness. They contended that current accounting systems do not provide this information, which is necessary for assessing the market risk determined value of a firm.

Rosenfield, Paul. "Reporting Subjective Gains and Losses." *Accounting Review*, October 1969: 788–97.

This examination of the concept of intertemporal and subjective gains and losses used them to evaluate the replacement price principle. The author concluded that the replacement price does not reflect opportunity cost and is therefore not relevant in preparing financial statements.

Rue, Joseph C., and David E. Tosh. "Continuing Unresolved Issues of Pension Accounting." *Accounting Horizons*, December 1987: 21–27.

The purpose of this paper was to explore some of the theoretical and reporting problems associated with the pension accounting arising under *FSAS no. 87.* The proposed measurement and recognition of both the pension obligation and the related intangible asset were questioned, and it was concluded that the *Standard* has some reporting requirements which are difficult to defend on either strict theoretical or practical grounds.

Schuetze, Walter. "Disclosure and the Impairment Question." *Journal of Accountancy*, December 1987: 26–32.

This paper reviewed problems in current practice about when to recognize "impairment" of long-lived, nonmonetary assets. One of the practical problems is, how should write-downs to recognize impairments be measured? Should discounted future cash flows be used? If so, what should be the discount rate?

Seaman, Jerome F., and Harold H. Hensald, Jr. "Pension Plan Obligations: The 'Real' Impact." *Journal of Accountancy*, July 1982: 82–88.

This was a review of *SFAS no. 35: Accounting and Reporting by Defined Benefit Pension Plans*, and *SFAS no. 36: Disclosure of Pension Information.* It concluded that these standards don't provide the minimum disclosure of future requirements to fulfill total pension plan obligations. The authors proposed disclosure of more comprehensive financial information about the funding status and the future funding requirements in the plan's financial statements and in footnotes to the plan's sponsor's financial statements.

Shannon, Donald, and William Stevens. "How Debt Refunding Can Cause Decision Conflicts." *Management Accounting*, December 1983: 40–44.

Bonds are initially recorded at their present value (market value), and any premium or discount recorded is amortized over the life of the issue. Subsequent to the date of issue, the market value of the bond is not recognized and therefore the economic reality is not recognized. Thus, upon early extinguishment of the debt an extraordinary gain or loss is recognized. The authors argued that a more relevant method, one that recognizes economic reality, needs to be used, and that this would improve financial reporting and remove a serious motivational conflict from management when a decision about early extinguishment of the debt is made.

Solomons, David. "The Determination of Asset Values." *Journal of Business* 35, no. 1 (January 1962): 28–42.

Solomon related the market value of used assets to the present value of future benefits and found that, in the presence of interest costs and taxes, used assets are more valuable than similar new assets in terms of their present values of future benefits.

Staubus, George J. "Letters to the Journal." *Journal of Accountancy*, July 1965: 17–19.

The author used the "Letters to the Journal" column to comment on Felix Kollaritsch's article, "Future Service Potential Value," qv. There were two features of this article with which he disagreed: one was the attempt to calculate the future cash flow of one part of a multipart productive facility; the other was the sweeping conclusion based on one example. The author concluded that the measurement of assets and liabilities by discounting anticipated cash flows is just one of the several useful methods of measurement accountants should and do employ.

———. "Current Cash Equivalent for Assets: A Dissent." *Accounting Review* 42, no. 4 (October 1967): 650–61.

Staubus analyzed selected decision situations in an attempt to determine which method of asset measurement could be expected to provide the most relevant information. He concluded that managers and investors have an interest in the maximum time-adjusted cash potential.

———. "The Measurement of Assets and Liabilities." *Accounting & Business Research*, no. 3 (Autumn 1973): 243–62.

Staubus contended that a set of criteria of useful financial information should be used by the accountant in choosing the best measurement method to use in a specific situation. The author thought that there are estimates of a common property, namely, discounted future cash flow. The author took the position that discounted future cash flow data are always more relevant to cash flow oriented decisions than is the data produced when any of the lower-ranking methods are used. He also contends that the discounted future cash flow method is generally the most relevant method for non-cash items.

———. "An Induced Theory of Accounting Measurement." *Accounting Review* 60, no. 1 (January 1985): 53–75.

This descriptive theory of accounting measurement remains one of the most comprehensive works on the theory of accounting measurement that has been published. Among other issues, Staubus examined specific measurement practices to ascertain what measurement methods are used and the qualities characterizing those methods. He identified eight basic measurement methods in current use: current market price, future cash flows, present value of future cash flows, net realizable value, original acquisition cost, current acquisition cost, original proceeds and equity. Of these eight, he identified the present value of future cash flows as the most generally accepted accounting principle.

Stepp, James O."Deferred Taxes: The Discounting Controversy." *Journal of Accountancy*, November 1985: 98–108.

This review of the issue of discounting deferred taxes concluded against discounting, for conceptual reasons and because of problems in application.

Sterling, Robert R. "Conservatism: The Fundamental Principle of Valuation in Traditional Accounting." *Abacus* 3, no. 2 (December 1967): 109–132.

Sterling observed that accounting is a discipline without any cohesive, unified theory of valuation because valuation methods vary widely for a wide variety of reasons, and indicated that present value is likely more objective than it is generally given credit for. Many accountants consider cost to be objective, but the author suspects that present values would vary less between firms than historical costs.

Stiner, Frederic M., and Roger Y. W. Tang. "The Controversy over Asset Valuation." *National Public Accountant* 21 (October 1976): 26–29.

The purpose of this article was to summarize and comment on the arguments relating to asset valuation methods; one of these methods being discounted cash flows. The authors recognized the contributions of George Staubus in having accountants recognize the relevance of present value in asset valuation and providing information of assistance in making economic decisions.

Thomas, Arthur L. "Discounted Services Again: The Homogeneity Problem." *Accounting Review* 39, no. 1 (January 1964): 1–11.

Thomas attempted an in-depth review of the valuation of assets in terms of the net discounted cash flows that they are expected to generate over their productive lives. He concluded that, because of the severe flaws of the discounted services approach, this valuation could contribute very little to financial accounting, although it could be used in limited situations such as the valuation of receivables and other cash claims.

Thomsen, C. Torben. "Dangers in Discounting." *Management Accounting*, January 1984: 37–39.

The author discussed time distortions induced by discounting and made the point that, by understanding time distortions introduced by discounting, the user of present value calculations can guard against applying discounting when it is not warranted. When discount rates are high, the time horizon becomes biased toward the near term. This can have a destablizing influence in the economy, which can make the short run more unstable. The author contended that it is unrealistic to assume that high interest rates (discount rates) can continue over an extended period of time.

Upton, Wayne S., and Mark V. Sever. "UL [Universal Life] Accounting Revisited." *Best's Review*, March 1987: 26–28.

This review of the proposed accounting for universal life-type insurance contracts noted that the FASB views universal life-type contracts as different from traditional insurance. The FASB believes that a liability measurement method based on the contract is more appropriate than one based on estimated cash flows. *SFAS no. 60: Accounting and Reporting by Insurance Enterprises* provides for a liability based on the present value of future benefits to policy holders and related expenses, less the present value of estimated future net premiums. The authors also noted that, in *SFAS 60*, the acquisition cost of deferred policies represents the present value of the portion of future gross premiums required to provide for the expenses of the book of contracts.

Wang, Penelope. "LA Accounting." *Forbes*, March 1988: 144–46.

This article was a review of the problem of how to modernize accounting rules to take account of all the new and complex financial instruments that have been invented in recent years. Bankers were especially upset over an FASB exposure draft that proposed that all financial institutions disclose the market value of their assets and liabilities in footnotes.

Warrell, C. J. "The Enterprise Value Concept of Asset Valuation." *Accounting & Business Research*, no. 2 (Summer 1974): 220–26.

Warrell maintained that a more satisfactory basis of valuation than historical cost is needed and suggested an enterprise value concept. The author commented that, when we consider the value of the enterprise, the appropriate figure is the expected future net receipts discounted by probability and interest factors to their present worth. But to apply this approach to an individual asset is to confuse two qualities relating to the asset: the value to the enterprise of the mere possession and the value to the enterprise of the efficiency with which the asset is expected to be used. This paper suggests a marginal analysis in which the value of an asset to an enterprise is equal to the decrement in the total value of the enterprise arising from the removal of that asset from the group.

Warshawsky, Mark J. "The Funding of Private Pension Plans." *Federal Reserve Bulletin*, November 1986: 853–54.

This was a summary of a study done by the staffs of the Board of Governors of the Federal Reserve System and of the Federal Reserve Banks on the funding of private pension plans. A major finding was that the general perception of an ongoing and robust improvement in the financial health of private pension plans was incorrect: pension plans were, on average, underfunded and their financial health had improved only slightly in 1981 to 1985.

Williams, Edward E., and M. Chapman Findlay, III. "Discounting Deferred Tax Liabilities: Some Clarifying Comments." *Journal of Business, Finance & Accounting* 2, no. 1 (Spring 1975): 121–33.

This article was a follow-up to Hugo Nurnberg's:, "Discounting Deferred Tax Liabilities," qv. The authors agreed with Nurnberg's position that deferred taxes represent an interest-free loan from the government which should increase net worth and be reported in income, but took exception with Nurnberg in several respects. They took the position that the discount rate should be the cost of equity times 1–t. Other issues that they took exception to are determining the amount of extra reported income and accounting for the distribution.

Wolk, Harry I., Lynn K. Saubert, and Frank M. Tiernan. "A Further Note On Discounting Deferred Taxes." *Journal of Business Finance & Accounting* 11, no. 2, (Summer 1984): 253-255.

The authors review the issue of whether the before-tax or after-tax rates should be used for discounting in financial accounting. The authors conclude that the before-tax rate is less ambiguous and simpler.

———, and Michael G. Tearney. "Discounting Deferred Tax Liabilities: Review and Analysis." *Journal of Business Finance & Accounting* 7, no.1 (Spring 1980): 119–33.

This article was a review of issues related to the discounting of deferred tax liabilities. The authors contended that deferred taxes are a liability and that the appropriate discount rate "would appear to be the rate applicable to an unsecured rate of similar maturity with a premium added for uncertainty."

Wyatt, Arthur R. "Leases Should Be Capitalized." *CPA Journal,* September 1974: 35–38.

The author demonstrated the case for capitalization of leases, noting that those who oppose capitalization often inject secondary considerations. He did not address what interest rate should be used.

Zeff, Stephen A. "Replacement Cost: Member of the Family, Welcome Guest, or Intruder?" *Accounting Review* 37, no. 3 (October 1962): 611–25.

This paper was an examination of the rate of replacement cost in financial reporting. In the determination of profit the author noted that J. R. Hicks's definition—a man's income is "the maximum value which he can consume during a week, and still expect to be as well off at the end of the week as he was at the beginning"—recurs frequently in economic and accounting writings. The "well-offness" of a firm was defined with reference to the discounted value of future net receipts.

Books

Beaver, William H. *Financial Reporting: An Accounting Revolution*, Englewood Cliffs, N.J.: Prentice-Hall, 1981.

Beaver commented that the notion that financial statement data ought to provide useful information about future cash flows appears to be relatively innocuous. He questioned this notion for two reasons: one, the concept of economic income is not well-defined when there are imperfect markets; second, when the relevant markets for claims exist, there has been an inability to reach a consensus on the "best" method of reporting.

Belkaoui, Ahmed. *Accounting Theory.* New York: Harcourt Brace Jovanovich, 1981.

Belkaoui observed that the concept of the maintenance of productive capacity requires the use of current values for assets and liabilities. He noted that there are several methods of calculating current value: (1) present value, (2) current entry price, (3) current exit price, and (4) a combination of values arrived at by the first three methods. He noted that present value income is a total, pure profit income expected to be accruing up to the firm's planning horizon. Such an income is an ex ante income that reflects expectations about future cash flows and can be computed when the relevant variables are known with certainty or in a situation in which all of the relevant variables are probabilistic. He observed that most authors define the discount rate as the subjective rate of return, but that several appropriate discount rates may be used to compute capitalized value, others being: (1) the historical rate of discount, (2) the current rate of discount, (3) the average expected rate of discount, (4) the weighted average cost of capital, and (5) the incremental borrowing rate.

Canning, John B. *The Economics of Accountancy*. New York: Ronald Press, 1929.

This work by John Canning is credited with linking interest and present value to accounting. (The work of the economist Irving Fisher is credited with influencing Canning in his application of present value to accounting.) Chapter 8, "The Measurement of Income," is a comparison and contrast of the accountant's theory of income with the economist's theory of income. It was Canning's opinion that the most extensive and articulated discussion of income in economic literature was in the writings of Irving Fisher. He observed that one apparent difference between the accountant's and Fisher's theory of income was Fisher's more complete "conceptual" accounting. Fisher described schematically how the "natural" uses of capital succeed one another in the many stages between primary origin and final use.

Chew, Donald H. *Six Roundtable Discussions of Corporate Finance with Joel Stern*. New York: Quorum Books, 1986.

The central theme in these discussions, moderated by Joel Stern, was market efficiency and the valuation by discounted cash flow. Joel Stern presented ideas about an economic model that holds "that the market value of corporate stock is the present value of a company's future expected after-tax free cash flow, discounted at rates which reflect investors' required returns for bearing risk. . . . When earnings seriously misrepresent operating cash flows, accounting statements distort performance and provide an unreliable guide to value"—p. 2. The economic model presented by Stern emphasizes cash flows and risk as measures of value and avoids bookkeeping entries that have no bearing on economic value.

Fisher, Irving. *Appreciation and Interest.* New York: Macmillan, 1986.

This book was published by Macmillan for the American Economic Association and is frequently cited in the literature. The author is Irving Fisher, an economist who is given a great deal of credit for advancing the concept of present value within the economic community. Chapter 4 "Present Value," introduced the concept. Two comments in this chapter are: (1) the literal meaning of "present value" implies that it is the actual market price today of a future sum due; and (2) the present value of a perpetual annuity is its "capitalized" value; thus, if the rate of interest is taken to be 5 percent, the present value of a perpetual annuity of $50 per annum is $1,000.

———. *The Theory of Interest.* New York: Macmillan, 1930.

This book was a rewrite with (new material) of Fisher's *The Rate of Interest*, which was published in 1907. The author was a highly recognized professor of economics at Yale University. The first chapter summarizes an even earlier work by Fisher called *The Nature of Capital and Income*, first published in 1906. *The Nature of Capital and Income* was a significant work on the relationship between capital and income. Chapter 2, "Money Interest and Real Interest," was a major contribution to the concept that money interest and real interest can be different and that, moreover, the money rate will be influenced by the appreciation or depreciation of goods. In chapter 17, Fisher tried to show that the theory of interest applies to every species of loan contract. The book concludes with chapter 21, a comprehensive summary of Fisher's theory of interest.

———. "Income and Capital." *In readings on the Concept and Measurement of Income*, edited by R. H. Parker, and G. C. Harcourt. Cambridge University Press. Cambridge: Cambridge University Press, 1969.

This is a summary of *The Nature of Capital and Income*, (1906) by economist Irving Fisher, a work given much credit as an early in-depth introduction of interest and present value. (Professor John B. Canning, an accountant, is given credit for extending Fisher's work to accounting.) Fisher concluded that the chief relations between capital and income are: (1) capital value is income capitalized or discounted; (2) if the rate of interest falls, the capital value (capitalized value of expected income) rises, and vice versa; (3) this rise or fall in capital value is relatively great for durable goods like land, and relatively small for transitory goods like clothes; (4) capital value is increased by savings, the income being decreased by the same account that the capital is increased; and (5) the savings thus diverted from income and turned back into capital will, except for mischance, be the basis for real income later.

Hendriksen, Eldon S. *Accounting Theory, Homewood.* Ill.: Richard D. Irwin, 1965.

This first edition of a major accounting theory text referenced John Canning's work as indicating that it would be desirable to have direct measures of all assets. Hendriksen concluded that this means that the best concept of valuation is one that is related to the expected future net receipt of funds. The degree of certainty involved in the estimate and the reliability of the estimation procedure govern the extent to which it can be applied. The text also references the Committee on Concepts and Standards Underlying Corporate Financial Statements of the American Accounting Association's 1957 *Statement* and *ARS no. 3* as supporting present value as a valuation concept. Hendriksen indicated that the present value concept requires knowledge of the amounts to be received, the discount factor, and the time periods involved, factors which may not be known with certainty. This leads to criticism of this method as being impracticable. Hendriksen indicated that statistical forecasting and probability techniques can often be used to convert uncertain future values into certain equivalents. He also noted that discounted cash flow applies to both assets and liabilities but that the amount of the discount may not be significant for short-term assets and liabilities.

Hicks, John R. *Value & Capital: An Inquiry into Some Fundamental Principles of Economic Theory*, 2d ed. (Oxford: Clarendon Press, 1946).

Part of the interest paid on securities is related to default risk, and part is attributed to uncertainty of the future course of interest. These can be viewed as risk elements. But Hicks left the impression that there must be more, other than these risk elements, to the determination of interest.

———. *In Readings on the Concept & Measurement of Income*, edited by R. H. Parker, and G. C. Harcourt. Cambridge: Cambridge University Press, 1969.

This selection, reprinted from his *Value and Capital* (qv.), contains Hick's often-quoted definitions of income. They are as follows: (1) income no. 1 is the maximum amount which can be spent during a period if there is to be an expectation of maintaining intact the capital value of prospective receipts in monetary terms, a definition that neglects interest; (2) income no. 2 is the maximum amount the individual can spend this week, and still expect to be able to spend the same amount in each ensuing week so long as the rate of interest is not expected to change, this definition comes to the same conclusion as the first but neglects price changes; (3) income no. 3 is the maximum amount of money which the individual can spend this week and still expect to be able to spend the same amount in real terms in each ensuing week (this definition assumes that interest rates reflect inflation rates perfectly).

———. *Capital and Time.* Oxford: Clarendon Press, 1973.

This is the third book that Hicks wrote about capital. The first, *Value and Capital* (1939), was a product of the Keynesian thirties. The second, *Capital and Growth* (1965), was critical and expository. It examined the variety of approaches from which the building of capital could be viewed. This, third, was evolved from the Austrian theory of Bhom-Bawerk and Hayek. Here, Hicks presented two caveats regarding the use of time value of money: first, that values calculated by using interest methods are not market values and that differences between the interest rate used in calculating present value and the actual rate of return will lead to discrepancies in the form of capital gains (losses); second, that time value is continuous while interest methods often involve the use of discrete intervals to calculate value.

Jaedicke, Robert K., and Robert T. Sprouse. *Accounting Flows: Income, Funds, and Cash.* Englewood Cliffs, N.J.: Prentice-Hall, 1965.

This book includes an examination of an economic concept of income based on the present value of future cash flows. The authors initially assumed conditions of certainty and that price levels do not change, unrealistic assumptions that the authors thought still gave some useful insight into the real nature of income. They used J. R. Hicks's definition of income as an ideal type of income concept—that is, that income is the "maximum value a man can consume during a week, and still expect to be as well off at the end of the week as he was at the beginning"—and felt that it applies to the firm even though it was stated in terms of the individual. They therefore restated the definition in terms of the firm, "as the maximum amount that could be distributed as dividends to shareholders without contraction of the firm's resources." The authors indicated that this concept of income could be implemented by calculating the present value of future cash flow at the beginning and end of the accounting period and by defining income as the difference between these two sums. They pointed out that, to the extent that the decision to purchase an asset is based on the present value of future cash inflows, a present value approach is used at acquisition. Thus, when a long-term bond is recorded on the basis of the proceeds at issuance, it is being recorded at present value. But once the original transaction is recognized, accountants do not typically consider a present value: for example, the fixed asset is depreciated without considering its present value.

Kam, Vernon. *Accounting Theory.* New York: Wiley, 1986.

In Kam's discussion of asset and liability measurement, present value is discussed as an approach that approximates true value. It is noted that Irving Fisher is credited with formulating the present value concept in a way that is serviceable to accountants; however, John Canning is credited with demonstrating the relationship of present value to the related future cash flow. When using present value, Kam wrote, the quantity of money is different but the "value" preference is the same because of the time dimension. The theory has gained wide acceptance because its premise appears to be true and because it appears that rational people in business behave in the way assumed by the theory. It appears that the present value method is an ideal approach for ascertaining value. The author also observed that the present value approach can be used for financial reporting purposes, but that its use is limited because the future cash flow of most nonmonetary assets is difficult to ascertain. While the net cash receipts of a firm are generated by the utilization of all the assets, it would be arbitrary to allocate certain amounts to each fixed asset.

Keller, Thomas F. *Accounting for Income Taxes.* Ann Arbor: Bureau of Business Research, University of Michigan Press, 1961.

This book was a survey of the issues related to accounting for income taxes, including their interperiod allocation. It includes a discussion of the difficulty of measuring the appropriate discount rate to be used in making such interperiod allocations.

Keynes, John Maynard. *General Theory of Employment, Interest, and Money.* New York: Harcourt Brace Jovanovich, 1936.

According to Keynes, interest is the premium on current cash over deferred cash, and measures the marginal preference for holding cash over deferred delivery. Interest, he believed, measures the marginal efficiency of money measured in terms of itself as a unit and an investment yields prospective returns, which are a series of annuities called "the prospective yield of the investment."

Leake, Pearcy D. *Depreciation and Wasting Assets and Their Treatment in Computing Annual Profit and Loss.* London: Henry Good, 1912.

In chapter 5, "The Interest Question," Leake described and analyzed two methods of making provision for expired capital outlay (depreciation) which involve the use of interest: one, the annuity method; the other, the sinking fund method. Leake concluded that these methods should never be used for measuring depreciation unless some special reason exists. He argued that, indiscriminate use of internal annual interest in connection with depreciation is often misleading and should be discouraged.

Lee, T. A. *Income and Value Measurement: The Practice.* Baltimore: University Park Press, 1975.

The fundamental relationship between income and capital was reviewed by Lee. He pointed out that, in accounting, capital and income are regarded as a stock and a flow, the stock (the balance sheet) resulting from a transacted flow which is accounted for when measuring accounting income. The stock-flow also exists in economics through the valuation of capital as a discounted future stream of income, income being the expired portion of capital. Fisher, who regarded interest as the bridge between the two concepts, is given credit for a rigorous examination of the relationship between income and capital.

Moonitz, Maurice. "Accounting for Investment in Debt Securities." In *Essays in Honor of William A. Paton*, edited by Stephen A. Zeff, Joel Demski, and Nicholas Dopuch (Ann Arbor: University of Michigan Press, 1979).

Moonitz discussed the consistent use of market values in accounting for debt securities, noting that the effect of changing interest rates on present values create two accounting issues: "when to recognize and report realized (explicit) holding gains (losses); and when to recognize and report the unrealized (implicit) holding gains (losses)." The author contended that realized income and unrealized gains (losses) should not be combined in the income statement.

———, and Louis H. Jordan. *Accounting: An Analysis of Its Problems.* New York: Holt, Rinehart & Winston, 1963.

The authors examined issues related to the valuation of assets and liabilities as well as the determination of periodic profits. Issues discussed include the use of discounting in amortizing bond discounts (premiums) and the types of uncertainty in accounting transactions and their effects on valuation. Types of uncertainties discussed include the ability of debtors to keep their promise, the appropriate discount rate to be used, the size and timing of future money flows, and the uncertainty created by the inability to apply direct valuation techniques. The authors recommended that the annuity method be used to allocate depreciation.

Most, Kenneth S. *Accounting Theory.* Columbus: Grid, 1977.

The author recognized that, in 1929, John B. Canning tried to establish accounting as a science in the mold of economics and regarded him as a disciple of the noted economist Irving Fisher. He also noted that Fisher achieved a superficial resemblance to accounting by relating income closely to property. Fisher's ideal income was the algebraic sum of expected net receipts from a specific property; Canning extended this to cover changes in value during the life of the property. Many definitions and concepts used by economists have been taken over by accountants, including present value. One of the crucial elements in determining present value is the discount factor. The author observed that Fisher viewed discount as the marginal rate at which society will substitute future for present satisfactions. It was long believed that the equivalent concept for a firm was the cost of capital, but most commented that the prevailing view when he wrote was that the appropriate discount rate is a risk-adjusted rate of interest. Most indicated that there are at least six valuation measures which could be used in current value accounting: (1) replacement cost, (2) net realizable value, (3) present value, (4) replacement value, (5) potential proceeds of sale, and (6) distress proceeds. He indicated that one of the problems of current value accounting is the necessity of expressing liabilities at present value, because, as interest rates rise, the present value of the liability falls. The change in present value between periods will increase income.

O'Driscoll, Gerald P., and Mario J. Rizzo. *The Economics of Time and Ignorance.* New York: Basil Blackwell, 1985.

These authors recognized that market participants are not indifferent to time considerations. The market systematically discounts the future and, as a result, the sum of the inputs falls short of the anticipated output by the extent of the time discount. Systematic discounting gives rise to the market phenomenon that may be seen as value productivity.

Paton, William A. *Accounting Theory.* New York: Ronald Press, 1922.

This book reviewed discounts on contractual securities, such as original issue discount on bonds. Paton's position was that the discount is an offset to the liability, because it represents interest which will be paid. The discount should be systematically accumulated so that the difference between the liability and the discount may express the true effective liability.

———. *Accountants' Handbook,* 3d ed. New York: Ronald Press, 1943.

Paton reviewed the interest method of depreciation. He held that interest is a factor in the cost of a fixed asset. Therefore, the revenue realized from the use of the fixed asset should include the interest earned on the remaining value of the investment (the theory behind the annuity method of depreciation).

Revsine, Lawrence. *Replacement Cost Accounting.* Englewood Cliffs, N.J.: Prentice-Hall, 1973.

Revsine discussed a normative investor model. In this model, the primacy of cash flow potential is emphasized, which suggests that investors are primarily concerned with the level and timing of future cash flow. Thus, to be relevant to decision making, accounting data must provide some reasonable basis for estimating future returns and their variability. The normative investor model states that an investor is primarily interested in estimating the future flow of dividends and the risk inherent in that flow. Accounting measurements should facilitate estimates of the flow and its associated risk, and this should be the primary criterion by which the relevance of the replacement cost to investors is to be judged.

Schroeder, Richard G., Levis D. McCullers, and Myrtle Clark. *Accounting Theory.* New York: Wiley, 1987.

The authors noted that many different measurement techniques are used when valuing assets on the typical balance sheet. Examples are cash (current value), accounts receivable (expected realizable value), marketable securities (lower of cost or market), inventory (lower of cost or market), investment (lower of cost, market, or historical cost), and plant and equipment (historical cost minus accumulated depreciation). The authors noted that summing these items is much like adding apples and oranges, and that a presentation of information about the expected future benefits would seem more appropriate. It was noted that current liabilities are usually measured at liquidation value, ignoring the time value of money, that long-term liabilities are frequently measured at present value, using the yield rate at the date of issue, and that liability valuations are not changed to reflect changes in the market rates of interest.

Smith, Adam. *An Inquiry Into the Nature and Causes of the Wealth of Nations,* Book 11. London: Oxford University Press, 1928.

In chapter 4, "Of Stock Lent at Interest," Smith commented on the role of interest in determining the market value of land. The ordinary market price of land depends on the ordinary market rate of interest. The higher the interest, the lower the common price of land; the lower the interest, the higher the common price of land. The person with capital deliberates whether to buy land or lend the capital out at interest.

Stanley, Curtis H. *Objectivity in Accounting.* Ann Arbor: University of Michigan Press, 1965.

In this book, Curtis introduced the concept of use value of an asset to a firm. It was based on the idea that each potential user of an item makes a return calculation to determine what value the item will provide in use. For a firm, this is the future net receipts, which are discounted to their present equivalent. Liabilities would be stated in terms of their present exit-market value, which would be the present number of dollars required to satisfy the liability (the present value of the amount required to satisfy the liabilities at their due dates). The author indicated that the required interest rate used for discounting would be influenced by several factors. The rate has a subjective sense, it is a community rate, and it is adjusted for uncertainties.

Staubus, George J. *A Theory of Accounting to Investors.* Berkeley: University of California Press, 1961.

Here, Staubus concentrated on the problems of investors, which include the nature of the investment decision and the information needed to make one. He developed a plan for measuring and classifying economic events. It was his view that measurement methods must have relevance to the firm's future cash flows, and that financial statements, in order to have value to the investor, should present evidence of the firm's future capacity to pay investors. An emphasis on future cash receipts and disbursements was the theme as assets, liabilities, revenues, and expenses were addressed. This is one of the most significant works that emphasized the importance of cash flow in the measurement process.

———. "The Relevance of Evidence of Cash Flows" In *Asset Valuation and Income Determination*, edited by Robert R. Sterling (Lawrence, Kans.: Scholars Book Co., 1970).

Staubus's hypothesis was "that the property of an asset or a liability that is most frequently relevant to the decisions for which accounting data are helpful is the difference in the present value of the firm's future cash flows that will result from the existence of the asset or liability. He also held that the most useful meaning of an asset or liability is the item's incremental effect upon the net discounted amount of the entity's future cash flows.

Sterling, Robert R. *Asset Valuation and Income Determination.* Lawrence, Kans.: Scholars Book Co., 1970.

This book includes papers presented at a symposium on asset valuation and income determination. One of the schools of thought, emphasizing discounted cash flows and economic income, was represented by George Staubus's "The Relevance of Evidence of Cash Flows." Staubus's hypothesis was "that the property of an asset or a liability that is most frequently relevant to the decisions for which accounting data are helpful is the difference in the present value of the firm's future cash flows that will result from the existence of the asset or liability." He also declared that "The most useful meaning of asset and liability quantities is the item's incremental effect upon the net discounted amount of the entity's future cash flows."

———. *Theory of the Measurement of Enterprise Income.* Lawrence, Kans.: University Press of Kansas, 1970.

As its title indicates, this book was a review of the theory of the measurement of enterprise income. It indicated a concurrence of opinion about the concept of income among economists as well as between economists and accountants, and that the problem was not with the definition of income but with the application of the concept of income . The author concluded that the basic disagreement centered around the phrase "as well off" in the definition. One of the approaches to the measurement of how "well off" a person or enterprise is came from Irving Fisher, whose approach was stated by Edgar O. Edwards and Philip W. Bell as follows: "In the absence of dividend payments and new contributions by stockholders, income is measured at the end of the period by adding up the discounted values of all net receipts which the managers then expect to earn on the firm's existing net assets and subtracting from this subjective value a similar computation made at the beginning of the period." (Edgar O. Edwards and Philip W. Bell, *The Theory and Measurement of Business Income,* Berkeley, California: University of California Press, 1961, 24-25) Sterling indicated that the usual criticism of this concept was its subjectivity and the uncertainty of the future .

Tinker, Tony. *Paper Prophets: A Social Critique of Accounting.* New York: Praeger Scientific, 1985.

Capitalism was defined by Tinker as a social system with conflict, who viewed capitalists as appropriating from the production process without giving anything in return. Thus, the time value of assets (liabilities) may be based on their productive capabilities (opportunity costs) when used by labor.

Wolk, Harry I., Jere R. Francis, and Michael G. Tearney. *Accounting Theory.* Boston: Kent Publishing, 1984.

Discounted cash flows were discussed here under current value systems, and the authors of this book had a negative opinion of the practicality of using discounted cash flows as a value system. They regarded it as a theoretical method with virtually no practicability on a statement-wide basis. They indicated that, when cash flow is discounted, both asset valuation and income measurement are anchored to future expectations. A problem with using discounted cash flows is that many assets contribute to the production of cash flows; another formidable problem is the estimation of future cash flows. The authors concluded that discounted cash flow can be used only for a very restricted group of assets and liabilities whose interest and principal payments are directly stipulated or can be imputed. George Staubus is referenced as advocating a substitute approach whereby assets would be valued in terms of those attributes assumed to approximate most closely their discounted cash flows in terms of their expected use. The authors observed that this results in a mixed bag of discounted cash flows, net realizable values, and replacement costs. They also observed that, because of the wide variation in asset realization and measurement, it is very difficult to interpret assets in the aggregate, and that the current balance sheet is impaired because of the additivity problem, which detracts from relevance or usefulness. The authors did not explain why using discounted cash flows would add to the current additivity problem.

Reports and Studies

Accounting Principles Board, (APB). *Statement no. 4: Basic Concepts and Accounting Principles Underlying Financial Statements of Business Enterprises*. New York: American Institute of Certified Public Accountants (AICPA), 1970.

The purpose of the statement was to provide a basis for guiding the future development of financial accounting. The present value concept was used in several areas, including money prices in measuring resources in financial accounting, and principles that guide the selection of events and assignment of dollar amounts.

Black, Homer A. *Interperiod Allocation of Corporate Income Taxes: Accounting Research Study [ARS], no. 9*. New York: AICPA, 1966.

This study recognized that, in theory, discounting was relevant to all assets and liabilities recognized by tax allocation procedure but that, as a practical matter, discounting is most likely to be applied to long-term liabilities. The study concluded that the arguments against discounting are not convincing. Accountants do account for present values of long-term liabilities and assets, and the argument of practicability was not regarded as to likely be valid. As to the discount rate, an appropriate rate can be selected once it is decided to discount.

Committee on Accounting Concepts and Standards. *Accounting and Reporting Standards for Corporate Financial Statements and Preceding Statements and Supplements,* Columbus: American Accounting Association (AAA), 1957.

This AAA's committee report suggested that present worth is the ideal guide to the measurement of an asset:

"The value of an asset is the money-equivalent of its service potentials. Conceptually, this is the sum of the future market prices of all streams of service to be derived, discounted by probability and interest factors to their present worth. However, the conception of value is an abstraction which yields but limited practical basis for quantification. Consequently, the measurement of assets is commonly made by other more feasible methods. Monetary assets—cash or claims to cash—should be expressed in terms of expected cash receipts adjusted for collection delay where significant. Cash on hand, demand deposits, and short-term government receivables are readily expressed in such terms because the force of interest and the uncertainty of collection are negligible. Other claims to cash may require adjustment to measure current realizable amounts. Accounts or notes receivable should be discounted for stated or implied interest factors, if material; they should also be reduced by allowances to cover shrinkage on collection. Still other cash claims may involve equitable consideration, as in the measurement of receivables arising from long-term construction contracts on a percentage of completion basis. In every case, however, the amount of monetary assets should be based on discernible, measurable, and reasonably certain collection and availability of cash"—p. 4.

Committee on External Reporting, AAA. *An Evaluation of External Reporting Practices: A Report of the 1966–68 Committee on External Reporting. Accounting Review*, Suppl. to vol. 44 (1969): 79–123.

This committee report suggested that the present value view of securities is widely accepted for investors' interest in the firm's future cash flows. The committee arrived at a dividend prediction model that emphasized the firm's future cash flows from continued operations and from changes in its asset and liability positions. This report lent support to the position that the present value of the future cash flows related to assets and liabilities is most relevant to decisions about securities investment .

Financial Accounting Standards Board (FASB). *Statement of Financial Accounting Concepts, no. 1: Objectives of Financial Reporting by Business Enterprises*. Stamford, Conn.: FASB, 1978.

Statement of Concept no. 1 noted that the discounted amount of future cash payments required by a long-term debt is the present value of the liability— par. 21.

———. *Statement of Financial Accounting Concepts, no. 2: Qualitative Characteristics of Accounting Information*. Stamford, Conn.: FASB, 1980.

Statement of Concept no. 2 noted that a choice must be made of the attribute of assets to be measured, these attributes being historical cost, current cost, current exit value, net realizable value, or present value of expected cash flows— par. 8.

———. *Statement of Financial Accounting Concepts, no. 5: Recognition and Measurement in Financial Statements of Business Enterprises*. Stamford, Conn.: FASB, 1984.

Statement of Concept no. 5 noted that items currently reported in the financial statements are measured by different attributes depending on the nature of the item and the relevance and reliability of the attribute measured. One of the attributes recognized was present value of future cash flows.

———. *Statement of Financial Accounting Concepts, no. 6: Elements of Financial Statements.* Stamford, Conn.: FASB, 1985.

This statement defined the elements of financial statements. The use of present value is recognized for some elements, such as bond investments and bonds payable.

Grady, Paul. *Inventory of Generally Accepted Accounting Principles: ARS, no. 7.* New York: AICPA, 1965.

This study was concerned with the concepts related to principles and practices which had general acceptance in 1965. Two areas were identified that used present value: one was the capitalization of leases when the lease was in effect an installment purchase of fixed assets; the other was recording a bond payable at the present value of the obligation on the date of issue.

Insurance Companies Committee, Auditing Standards Division. *Discounting Claim Liabilities of Insurance Companies*. New York: AICPA, 1982.

The AICPA's Insurance committee prepared this report in the process of revising the AICPA's industry guide, *Audits of Fire and Casualty Insurance Companies.* The committee identified several accounting issues that were not discussed in the audit guide or about which existing practice varied. One was whether claim liabilities should be discounted. Since that issue also exists in life, health, title, and mortgage guarantee insurance companies, it was addressed from an overall standpoint. The committee concluded that claim liabilities should be recorded at the present value of anticipated net cash payments if the net payment pattern and ultimate cost are fixed or reasonably determinable on either an individual or group basis—par. 32. The interest rate used to discount claim liabilities should be the pre-tax yield expected to be earned on total invested assets over the period that the claim liabilities are expected to be paid—par. 48.

Johnson, L. Todd, and Reed K. Storey. *Recognition in Financial Statements: Underlying Concepts and Practical Conventions*. Stamford, Conn.: FASB, 1982.

This FASB research report was prepared as part of its accounting recognition project, a project intended to provide conceptual guidance on when and how to recognize the effect of transactions and other events on an entity's assets, liabilities, and equity. Several areas in the report relate to cash flow and present value, including:

1. The value of an asset or a liability. "The value of an asset (or group of assets) or a liability (or group of liabilities) at any time is equal to its present cash consequence (which is the same as its future cash consequences discounted to the present or its past cash consequences accumulated to the present)—pp. 37–38.
2. Income. "Over the life of a business enterprise, its comprehensive income equals the net of its cash inflows and cash outflows, excluding cash investments by owners and cash distributions to owners"—p.39.
3. Rate of Return. "A rate of return on an asset reflects both the time value of money and the risk of holding the asset"—p. 58.

Lamden, Charles W., Dale L. Gerboth, and Thomas W. McRae. *Accounting Research Monograph, no. 1: Accounting for Depreciable Assets*. New York: AICPA, 1975.

In this monograph on accounting for depreciable assets, two depreciation methods are identified that are primarily based on the notion that some fixed rate of return should be realized on the investment in depreciable assets: the sinking-fund method and the annuity method. Both methods are based on an assumed fixed rate of return on the net investment in an asset. The empirical tests presented for determining the circumstances in which increasing-charge methods of depreciation are most appropriate are:

1. When the net-revenue contributions or operating efficiency of an asset is indeterminable or, to the extent determinable, tends to be constant or to increase with the age of the asset.

2. When the asset is used by an enterprise that is able to price its goods or services so as to obtain a fixed rate of return on investment (for example, when rates established by regulatory authorities).

3. When other asset-related charges are expected to be constant or to decrease over the estimated useful life of the asset—p. 102.

Moonitz, Maurice. *The Basic Postulates of Accounting: ARS, no. 1*, New York: AICPA, 1961.

The Special Committee on Research Program of the AICPA proposed that the basic postulates underlying accounting and of the broad principles of accounting be studied. These studies were intended to serve as the foundation for the entire body of future pronouncements by the APB. *ARS, no. 1* does not directly refer to using present value in financial reporting; the related study, *ARS* no. 3, does include the use of present value in financial reporting.

Ronen, Joshua. "Discounted Cash Flow Accounting." In *AICPA Objectives of Financial Statements, no. 2* , edited by J. J. Cramer and G. H. Sorter. New York: AICPA, 1974.

The authors of this conceptual approach to discounted cash flow accounting observed that, while the individual values assigned to assets and liabilities would not necessarily add up to the total value of the firm, the separate communication may be useful in evaluating the management of the individual assets and liabilities. There exist two quantifications of expected cash flow: the cash flow that is expected by the firm's management and the cash flow that is expected by all others.

———. "A Test of the Feasibility of Preparing Discounted Cash Flow Accounting Statements." In *AICPA Objectives of Financial Statements, no. 2* edited by J. J. Cramer and G. H. Sorter. New York: AICPA, 1974.

This examination of the feasibility of applying the discounted cash flow system of accounting to an actual firm was an attempt to provide some insight into the time and effort required to use such a system. The writer expressed the opinion that estimates of cash flows attributable to specific assets or groups of assets could be obtained with relatively small amounts of time and cost.

Sanders, Thomas H., Henry R. Hatfield, and U. Moore. *Statement of Accounting Principles*. New York: AAA, 1938.

In this *Statement*, reference is made to the accounting for bond discount: "the discount is in a sense an offset to the liability from which it arises, having the mathematical effect of reducing that liability to its present worth. But the practice is well established of showing the bond liability at its face value. When, therefore, the bonds are issued at a discount, a contra item is involved"—p. 78.

Scott, George M. *Research Study on Current-Value Accounting Measurements and Utility*. New York: Touche Ross Foundation, 1978.

Dr. George M. Scott of the University of Texas was the lead researcher in this study funded by the Touche Ross Foundation. A major finding was that current value measures are better predictors of future operating cash flows than is historical cost. It was shown that investors and creditors require accounting values about individual resources and obligation to help their prediction of company cash flows and liquidity. A number of advantages to management were indicated by measures of current value. Managers would be assisted in strategic planning, managerial control, operations control, and external relations. The INFLAN computer simulation model was used to examine the relationship of operating cash flows to historical cost net income and to various measures in conformance with the current value accounting model. There was strong evidence that at least one of the current value measurements examined outperforms historical cost net income as a predictor of the next year's operating cash flows in most of the wide variety of inflationary conditions simulated. The study concluded that discount rates should compensate for the time value of money, expected inflation, and risk. The discount rates should also encompass the term structure of interest rates that is appropriate for the particular resource. When present value cannot be reasonably estimated, a measurement approach should be used to establish a current-cost surrogate. A significant contribution of this study was the establishment of a cash flow prediction as a major purpose to which financial statements should be put.

Sprouse, Robert T., and Maurice Moonitz. *A Tentative Set of Broad Accounting Principles for Business Enterprises: ARS no. 3*. New York: AICPA, 1962.

This significant research report was intended to serve as part of the foundation for the entire body of future pronouncements by the APB. Chapter 4 describes the use of present value for money or claims to money. Chapter 5 describes the use of present value for the measurement of liabilities.

Study Group on the Objectives of Financial Statements. *Report of the Study Group on the Objectives of Financial Statements*. New York: AICPA, 1973.

This study group was organized to seek goals that related to information presented in financial statements. It concluded that the objectives of financial statements cannot be served by the exclusive use of a single valuation basis. The four valuation bases identified were historical cost, exit values, current replacement cost, and discounted cash flows.

Task Force on Impairment of Value, Accounting Standards Division, AICPA. *Issues Paper 83-2: Accounting for the Inability to Fully Recover the Carrying Amounts of Long-Lived Assets*. New York: AICPA, 1980.

An issue discussed is whether the inability to fully recover the carrying amounts of long-lived assets should be reported. Those against reporting indicated several problems including: (1) inaccuracies in forecasting cash flows, (2) ascribing revenue to a particular long-lived asset, and (3) the subjectivity of the discount rate. Various asset measurements were considered when the carrying amounts of long-lived assets cannot be recovered were considered: one was the net present value of expected future cash flows.

Task Force on Discounting Applications, Accounting Standards Division, AICPA. *Issues Paper 87-2: The Use of Discounting in Financial Reporting for Monetary Items with Uncertain Terms, Other than Those Covered by Existing Authoritative Literature*. New York: AICPA, 1987.

Discounting was approached in a general manner, with a focus on the loss reserve of property or casualty insurance enterprises and also on deferred income taxes. The first section of the paper addressed concepts of discounting as they relate to monetary items with uncertain terms. Some of the conclusions on the task force were:

1. *Cash flow*. The present value of future cash flows is the most relevant measurement attribute for the initial recognition of the monetary items with uncertain terms included within the scope of the paper.

2. *Discounting*. Discounts should be applied in the initial recognition of monetary items with uncertain terms when the amounts and timing of cash flows are reasonably estimable.

3. *Timing*. If a range of timing of cash flows is known or reasonably estimable, then the most likely data (or period) within that range should be used to compute the present value of future cash flows.

4. *Liabilities*. The discount rate should be objectively determinable and be the best estimate of the rate at which the monetary liabilities with uncertain terms could be settled or effectively settled.

5. *Assets or Receivables*. The discount rate should be objectively determin-

able and be the best estimate of the rate at which the monetary asset with uncertain terms could be sold.

6. *Discount Rate.* The discount rate used to determine the present value of future cash flows in the initial recognition of monetary items with uncertain terms (excluding deferred income tax assets and liabilities) should be a pre-tax rate.
7. *Changes in timing.* Changes in the estimates of the timing of cash flows occurring subsequent to the initial recording of monetary items with uncertain terms based on new facts should be recorded as a gain or loss in the income statement unless properly capitalized as part of the cost of an asset.
8. *Changes in the discount.* The majority of the task force members believed that changes in the discount rate occurring subsequent to the initial recording of the item should be assessed annually and recognized in the financial statements at that time.
9. *Growth in present value.* The accretion of the present value may be reflected as interest expense or interest income, as applicable, or may be combined with the event that gave rise to the accretion, with appropriate disclosure in the notes to the financial statements.

Wheeler, James E., and Willard H. Galliart. *An Appraisal of Interperiod Income Tax Allocation.* Morristown, N.J.: Financial Executives Research Foundation, 1974.

The authors discussed the possibility of presenting interperiod income tax allocation at the discounted amount. They recognized that there is a body of literature supporting the use of discounting for interperiod income tax allocation as a means of determining the "burden" of the tax deferral and as a means of allocating the tax cost between years. It was also noted that some of the leading critics of comprehensive tax allocation have supported discounting of deferred taxes. The authors supported a thorough consideration of the strengths and weaknesses of reporting deferred tax on a discounted basis. Such a review should take into account three factors: (1) what is to be discounted? (2) what is the length of the discount period? and (3) what rate is appropriate? After discussion, the authors concluded against discounting in each case. They also questioned the ability of readers of the financial statements to understand the significance of discounted deferred tax and thought that the resulting financial statements would be less valuable.